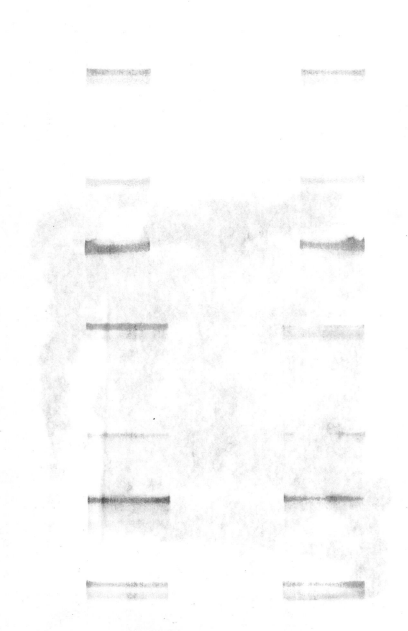

THE DARK EAGLE
The Story of
BENEDICT ARNOLD

Clifford Lindsey Alderman

921
Arn

MACMILLAN PUBLISHING CO., INC.

NEW YORK

For Jo-Ann Jordan

Macmillan Publishing Co., Inc.
866 Third Avenue, New York, N.Y. 10022
Collier Macmillan Canada, Ltd.
Map by Rafael Palacios
Printed in the United States of America
10   9   8   7   6   5   4   3   2   1

LIBRARY OF CONGRESS CATALOGING IN PUBLICATION DATA
Alderman, Clifford Lindsey.
    The dark eagle.

    SUMMARY: A biography of the ardent patriot and
brilliant general who became America's most infamous
traitor.
    Bibliography: p.
    Includes index.
    1.   Arnold, Benedict, 1741–1801—Juvenile literature.
[1.   Arnold, Benedict, 1741–1801.   2.   United States—
History—Revolution, 1775–1783—Biography]   I.   Title.
E278.A7A75   973.3′092′4 [B] [92]   75-40087
ISBN 0-02-700210-1

Contents

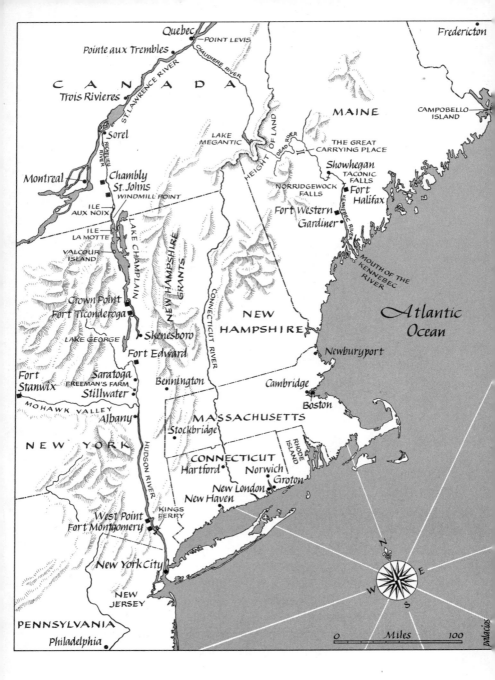

Prologue

Natanis, an Abnaki Indian chief, kept a close though secret eye on Benedict Arnold and his force of American soldiers during their famous march to Quebec in the winter of 1775. On at least one occasion during that desperate journey the Indians helped some of the Americans. However, Arnold himself did not like or trust Natanis at first, for after meeting the chief early in the march he suspected him of being a spy for the British.

While Arnold and his men were struggling to reach Quebec, Natanis is reported to have said: "The Dark Eagle [Arnold] comes to claim the wilderness. The wilderness will yield to the Dark Eagle but the Rock [Quebec] will defy him. The Dark Eagle will soar aloft to the sun. Nations will behold him and sound his praise. Yet when he soars the highest his fall is most certain. When his wings brush the sky then the arrow will pierce his heart."

Natanis's legendary assessment of Benedict Arnold came true. Not even the great sixteenth-century astrologer Nostradamus, some of whose predictions proved uncannily accurate, wrote a prophecy with more deadly precision.

This is the story of America's most infamous traitor, whose

heroic deeds before his treason are largely forgotten except by historians. He was probably the greatest fighting general America had before his attempt to sell out his country ended his service in the American Revolutionary army. George Washington, who is thought of as the greatest Revolutionary general, made several mistakes, some of them costly. Nathanael Greene, generally considered second only to Washington, made only one mistake, but it was so disastrous that the British might have won the war then and there if they had followed up their advantage quickly and with better strategy. Benedict Arnold, with one possible exception, made no errors during his service for America. It has not been proved, as will be explained later, that he was responsible for this error, and in any event it is not likely that it affected the outcome of the war.

Charles Dickens, in the opening paragraphs of his famous story *A Christmas Carol,* says: "Marley was dead, to begin with. There is no doubt whatsoever about that. . . . This must be perfectly understood or nothing wonderful can come of this story I am going to relate."

To paraphrase Dickens: Benedict Arnold was a traitor, to begin with. There is no doubt whatsoever about that. He came within a hair's breadth of successfully selling out his country to the British. In recent times some historians have argued that Arnold's treason should be forgiven and forgotten because of his heroism and earlier bold deeds in America's behalf.

It cannot be done. The treason is there, proved beyond the slightest doubt by the records. A man who tried to sell America back to Britain and end the desperate struggle of the American colonies for freedom should not be forgiven. Although Arnold had good reason to resent the shabby treatment he received from some generals and from the Continental Congress, this does not clear him of his guilt.

Benedict Arnold threw away everlasting glory and honor in exchange for a large sum of money. Throughout the rest of his life he was regarded with distrust by the men he had dealt with in his treason, and with scorn and shame by Americans and many British subjects. Truly, like Esau in the Old Testament, he had sold his birthright for a mess of pottage.

The purpose of this book is to describe the life of Benedict Arnold and to show how certain traits of his character enabled him to perform remarkable deeds in the service of his country, while others led him to become a traitor.

ONE

The Boy

He was the fifth Benedict Arnold of his family. Those before him were a mixed lot, ranging from a highly distinguished man, the first of the name, down through the traitor's father, who died a drunkard.

The first Benedict Arnold came to Rhode Island from England in 1635. A gifted man, he rose to become president of the colony in 1657, succeeding its founder, Roger Williams. When a royal charter was granted to Rhode Island in 1663, this first Benedict was elected its governor and served several terms in that post, dying in office in 1678.

His son, the second Benedict Arnold, did not turn out as well. He was a member of the Rhode Island Assembly for a time, but as a businessman he was unsuccessful. The third Benedict, the traitor's father, became well-off as a sea captain and merchant in Connecticut, but overfondness for rum and Madeira wine started his downward slide toward death. He had a son, Benedict, who died very young, and when another son was born on January 14, 1741, in the pretty little village of Norwich in eastern Connecticut, he was named Benedict for his dead brother and became the fifth of his name.

All was still well with the Arnold family as young Benedict

grew up to school age. His father had married his mother when she was Mrs. Hannah King, widow of a sea captain. Hannah King Arnold was a good woman, but she coddled and spoiled young Benedict.

As a young gentleman of means, Benedict was sent away to school. In 1752, at the age of eleven, he rode in a coach to the village of Canterbury, about fifteen miles north of Norwich on the Quinnebaug River. Canterbury was set among hills, charming with its village green, colonial New England meetinghouse and river flowing under a wooden bridge. It is not hard to picture Benedict alighting from the coach in his fine suit, white shirt with ruffles at the throat and cuffs and perhaps silver buckles on his knee breeches and boots, walking even then with the arrogant strut that was typical of him in later years.

He was enrolled in a boarding school run by the Reverend Dr. James Cogswell. Cogswell was a scholarly man, and the high reputation of his academy drew students from neighboring colonies, as well as Connecticut.

Benedict was then a high-spirited boy, cocksure of himself, hot-tempered and inclined to get into any adventure he could find. He was muscular, rather short, with black hair, dark complexion and light-colored eyes that had a look of coldness.

Little is known of his education at Canterbury except that he probably studied Latin, Greek, mathematics, public speaking and perhaps some Hebrew. Later in his civilian career he would pick up a knowledge of French that would stand him in good stead during his Revolutionary campaigns in Canada. What is better known is that he was a great show-off. When a building in Canterbury caught fire, Benedict climbed to the roof and disported himself, heedless of the flames below, to the awe of his classmates and the benefit of his conceit.

Benedict's mother tried to instill some of her own piousness into her son, but he resented it. When a letter from her dated April 12, 1754, arrived at the school, Benedict was more interested in the enclosure that came with it than in the letter itself. Nor did he mind his poorly educated mother's spelling in a postscript she added: "I have sent you 50s [50 shillings]. Your father put in 20 more. Youse itt prudently, as you are accountable to God and your father." If Benedict's use of any money that came his way in after years is any indication, he probably spent the gift immediately on sweets and other luxuries.

While Benedict was away, his father's drinking had increased so greatly that the family's money dwindled rapidly. In 1755 the lad had to be withdrawn from the Canterbury school.

He returned to Norwich, where for a year or two he idled about the wharves with playmates of his own age. His loafing was to be of value to him later on, however. Norwich was a seaport of sorts, at the head of navigation on the Thames River. Seagoing ships, mostly schooners and some of the smaller square-rigged vessels, loaded and discharged at the Norwich wharves. These ships traded largely with other American colonies, most often sailing to Boston, and sometimes with the West Indies, or Sugar Islands, as they were often called. Young Benedict came to know ships from stem to stern and main truck to keelson, along with the names and usage of every piece of cordage and canvas aboard them.

Benedict Arnold was still short and somewhat small for his

age; in fact, as a man he was not tall or large. But his body developed quickly. He could leap like a catamount, swim like a porpoise and dive like a loon. Above all, among the other boys, he was the leader in every adventure and demanded recognition of his abilities.

Benedict often gained that recognition by performing reckless deeds. As his playmates watched open-mouthed, he would leap into one of the buckets on the great water wheel of the gristmill, let himself be carried to the top, then down, and propelled into the millstream by the powerful thrust of the wheel.

When the Seven Years War, involving Britain against France, broke out in Europe, it spread quickly to the American colonies and Canada, where it was known as the French and Indian War. Word of a British victory reached Norwich, and Benedict decided that a celebration was called for. New England towns had stocks of arms, and there was a cannon in Norwich. Benedict stole some powder from the village magazine, filled a powder horn with it and poured it down the muzzle of the piece. Then he rammed in a flaming torch. He was lucky to escape from the explosion with only his hair singed.

Another time, Benedict proposed to his comrades that a holiday be celebrated properly with a big bonfire on the village green. So he led them to a wharf where they seized some barrels and began rolling them toward the green. The village constable promptly ordered them to return the barrels. The trigger-tempered Benedict whipped off his coat and offered to fight the policeman. The constable was a man who stood for no nonsense from young whippersnappers, however, so he collared Benedict and hauled him off home to his mother.

There were other pranks, and so Benedict Arnold's boyhood passed. Even at that time, his urge for distinction, arrogance toward others and love of money and good living stood out. Avarice would soon rule him in all his business dealings.

Business, for Benedict Arnold, was about to begin. He no longer enjoyed good living at home. Hannah Arnold was finding it more and more difficult to keep her family clothed and fed as her husband slipped further into alcoholism. She apprenticed Benedict to her cousins, David and Joshua Lathrop, apothecaries who dispensed pills and other medicines at a shop in the village. Benedict Arnold's boyhood was over.

TWO

Early Young Manhood

The Lathrop brothers were doing well. It is believed that their drugstore was the only one in Connecticut on the route between Boston and New York that ran through Norwich. Both apothecaries, or pharmacists, as they are generally called today, were graduates of Yale College, and David, the elder, had gone to London to learn the drug trade. They dealt not only in drugs, but in wines, dried fruits and some other merchandise they imported from Europe and India. When Benedict Arnold became their apprentice, fighting in the French and Indian War had begun and the Lathrops had a contract to furnish surgical equipment to the British and colonial troops in the Lake George battle zone.

In the dim, gloomy store, Arnold did all sorts of odd chores, sweeping, dusting and helping the two apothecaries in such tasks as could be done without expert knowledge. In this way he picked up a good deal of information about the trade that would later aid him in his own business. But he found it all insufferably dull and spent much of his time dreaming of the heroic deeds he would perform if only he could be a soldier fighting against the French from Canada.

Connecticut was in far less danger of invasion or raids by

the French and their allies of the Algonquin nation than were the frontiers of Massachusetts Bay, New York and Pennsylvania, yet it sent more than its share of troops to the Lake George area, where a campaign was in progress. Young Arnold followed the news of the war with intense interest. When a British recruiting officer's detachment in brilliant uniforms marched into Norwich one day to the cadence of a fife and drum corps, he ached to shed his knee-length working smock, rush out and beg to be enlisted. But he was still too young.

At last, in the spring of 1758, with the war approaching a climax, Arnold did not go to work one morning. Instead he set out over the rutted, sometimes dusty, sometimes miry road that led to New Haven and on to New York City. He might easily have enlisted at New Haven in a Connecticut regiment, but no doubt he knew that the New York colony paid higher bounties for recruits. Arnold was never one to overlook some extra shillings.

From New York City he went to Westchester County where, he had learned, a company was being raised to march toward Lake George. On March 30 he enlisted in the company, commanded by Captain Reuben Lockwood. Exactly what happened next is not fully clear, but apparently his mother, frantic over his disappearance, sought the aid of the Connecticut colony authorities in Hartford to have him sent back. Back he came, anyway, to the drudgery of the drugstore.

Such setbacks never discouraged Benedict Arnold. He pestered his mother continually to let him go to war. She finally yielded in 1759, when a two-pronged invasion, one prong aimed at Quebec and the other at Montreal, was being planned. Arnold returned to New York and enlisted in a company commanded by Captain James Holmes, an officer under whom he had served in Captain Lockwood's company. It marched to Fort Edward, a little south of Lake George, to join the army led by Lord Jeffrey Amherst.

There Arnold quickly learned that military service is not all pomp and glory. The first objective of the army was Fort Ticonderoga (then French-held and called Fort Carillon) on Lake Champlain. Such northward trails as there were had to be cleared and widened for the passage of artillery. Felling and hauling away huge trees and removing the deep-rooted, rock-hard stumps were sweaty, back-breaking tasks. Constant drilling and maneuvering and keeping quarters clean were wearisome and boring. This wasn't war, just drudgery.

Arnold wanted to leave, but desertion was a serious matter, especially in wartime. Then one day a letter came from Norwich saying his mother was ill. That night he sneaked out of camp and headed home. He accepted lifts from farmers and peddlers in wagons after looking them over warily and then carefully concealing his identity. At night he slept in barn haylofts.

The military authorities were after him. On May 21, 1759, an advertisement appeared in the *New York Gazette* describing him and offering a reward of forty shillings for his capture. But he reached home and found his mother feeling better. She hid him out during the summer of 1759 whenever recruiting officers were in Norwich.

Her illness recurred and grew worse that summer, and on August 15, Hannah King Arnold died. Arnold loved his mother, and her death left a lasting sense of loss in him. Even his father was so grief-stricken that he vowed never to touch liquor again, although he quickly forgot his promise. The

Arnold household was now dependent upon Arnold's sister, Hannah, a year younger than he, and the only other child of Hannah King Arnold's marriages. Tall and blonde, Hannah would be a pillar of strength to her brother throughout almost all of his life. She was capable, devoted and ready to sacrifice her own hopes and dreams for her family.

In spite of his disillusionment with his army service, the urge to be a soldier was still strong in Arnold. In September 1759, General James Wolfe captured Quebec after a great battle on the Plains of Abraham outside the city wall, a battle in which both he and the French commander, the Marquis de Montcalm, were mortally wounded. With this victory, the conquest of Canada by the British was virtually assured. All that remained was for Amherst to take weakly defended Montreal.

When the British general moved in the summer of 1760, Arnold was back in the colonial army. The authorities seem to have forgiven his desertion, for there is no record of any action being taken against him. But he saw no fighting. The French abandoned Carillon, Amherst took Montreal easily, and the war ended. After another dreary round of garrison duty, Arnold was released and sent home.

He then turned to his other love, the sea. He shipped out for the West Indies as a supercargo, in charge of cargo arrangements during the voyage. When he returned home, he began trading in a small way in several Connecticut ports and later journeyed to London, where he bought as much merchandise as he could afford, including drugs and books.

He had a business project in mind. When his father died of alcoholism in 1761, Arnold put his plan into effect. In that year he moved to Connecticut's richest and most flourishing town, New Haven. There he leased a store on one of the principal streets and filled it with the items he had bought in London.

It was one of the most unusual stores in America. Back in the nineteenth century, a drugstore was just that, unlike the modern ones that are almost small-scale department stores. Arnold's drugstore was probably the first in America to sell many things besides medicines. He had a large stock of books, including not only the latest best sellers from London, but classics, political and theological essays, poetry and what to-day are called "how-to-do-it" books, such as *Every Man His Own Lawyer* and *Ellis's Practical Farmer*. Students at Yale College in New Haven could buy Latin, Greek and French grammars. Arnold sold pictures, prints, maps, stationery, wall-paper and paints. There was a selection of cheap jewelry, buttons and buckles. Housewives could obtain figs, currants, the African fruit called tamarinds, and such spices and herbs as cinnamon, cloves, mace and rosemary.

In short, Arnold ran what was close to a combined pharmacy and general store. The sign over the door read:

B. ARNOLD
Druggist, Bookseller &c.
From London
Sibi Totique

The Latin phrase at the bottom meant "For himself and all"—especially himself. In those days a pharmacist needed no license, and Arnold prepared his pills and other medicines from the knowledge he had gained with the Lathrops in Norwich, although even then some preparations that later were known as "patent medicines" came already prepared. As still often happens in pharmacies today, customers were apt to call a pharmacist "doctor." Benedict Arnold enjoyed being addressed by the undeserved title of "Dr. Arnold."

His sister, Hannah, remained to keep up the house in Norwich. However, it is clear that Arnold assumed that he was head of that household as well. His arrogance and his often unreasoning hot temper are well illustrated by an occurrence during one of his frequent visits to the old home.

Although not beautiful, Hannah was intelligent, witty and had engaging manners. Arnold discovered that a young Frenchman, said to have been a dancing master, was wooing her. Arnold's lifelong dislike of Frenchmen probably stemmed from Puritan New England's aversion to Catholics, especially French-Canadian ones, as well as from the colonial wars against the French that had just ended. At any rate, Arnold ordered Hannah not to see the man again.

Hannah had some of Arnold's stubbornness. She ignored her brother's demand and continued to see the Frenchman, although only when she thought her brother would not be in Norwich. However, Arnold, with a companion, arrived unexpectedly one evening from New Haven. As they approached the door, Arnold saw in the candlelight from a front window that his sister was entertaining the Frenchman.

He told his acquaintance to knock at the door and enter immediately, as he himself would have done. He then drew a pistol, loaded it and waited in front of the house as the unexpected visitor entered. The startled Frenchman leaped in terror through the window. Arnold fired over the fellow's head. It was enough to convince the Frenchman that Norwich was not a healthy place for him, and he hastily departed.

Poor Hannah must have had a deep affection for her suitor,

for she was grief-stricken and resentful toward her domineering brother. Yet she not only forgave him but remained faithful and served him devotedly for many years before her death at the age of forty-four. She never married. And Arnold could never have achieved the financial success he did before the Revolution without her help.

He needed help now in running the New Haven store, since he was already expanding as a merchant, trading with the West Indies and Canada. Hannah came to New Haven, and in 1764 Arnold sold the Norwich house.

With his capable sister in the store, Arnold began to make trading voyages. It was an occupation in which toughness, shrewd business sense and little regard for fair dealing were essential. Arnold had all these qualities, and they brought him quick prosperity.

More than once in the years before the Revolution, Arnold's arrogance and short temper got him into difficulties. During a voyage to the Caribbean as captain of his own ship, the *Fortune*, he lay at anchor off a port on the Gulf of Honduras in Central America, taking on ginger and mahogany. Several other ships were also in the harbor. On such occasions it was traditional for the captains to get together in a convivial gathering aboard one of the ships. In this case the gathering was to be in a British vessel whose master was Captain Croskie, a crabbed old sea dog inclined to violent rage against anyone who failed to show him proper respect.

The *Fortune* was nearly ready to sail, and Arnold was busy with the ship's papers. With the last of the outward cargo coming aboard, he could not spare a single hand to row him over to Croskie's vessel. However, when loading was completed the next morning, he hastened over to call on the British shipmaster and offer regrets for missing the party.

After the many toasts drunk the evening before, Croskie may have had a headache that made him particularly mean-tempered. "You damned Yankee!" he shouted at his visitor. "Have you no manners?"

Arnold's short temper boiled over and he promptly challenged Croskie to a duel. Croskie accepted and the duel was fought on a small island in the bay. Croskie was late arriving and Arnold was about to leave, when not only the Britisher, his seconds and surgeon, but a number of natives approached in a boat. Scenting some sort of trickery, Arnold aimed his pistol at the boat and threatened to fire if it came nearer. He then allowed Croskie and his attendants to land but ordered the natives away until the fight was over.

With bad grace Croskie accepted Arnold's terms, but when, as the challenged man, he fired first, the bullet went wide. Although Arnold was a good shot, he was satisfied to have grazed Croskie's arm when he fired.

The British captain's wound was dressed, and the two duelists took up their positions again with reloaded pistols. By that time Croskie was in such a nervous state that when Arnold called out, "I give you notice, if you miss this time I shall kill you!" the Britisher apologized and Arnold accepted.

This was not the last time that Arnold's temper caused him trouble. His next difficulty stemmed from his involvement in molasses trading. British interference with this colonial venture was one of the underlying causes of the American Revolution. Molasses from the West Indies was one of the most important products imported by the New England colonies.

Dozens of distilleries were busy turning out rum from molasses, which was also made into sugar. In 1733 the British Parliament passed the Molasses Act, which placed a duty of sixpence a gallon on molasses imported from any port but a British one, in order to stop trading in molasses from French-owned West Indian islands. The New England merchant–shipowners paid no attention to the new law, and since Britain made no serious attempt to enforce it, trade with the French West Indies went on as usual.

But when the Molasses Act expired in 1763, Parliament passed the Sugar Act in 1764, cutting the duty on foreign molasses in half but at the same time providing measures to enforce the new law strictly. British West Indian sugar planters took advantage of the act by increasing prices for their molasses. New England distillers and sugar manufacturers found their profits reduced. So did farmers and other producers of exports to the West Indies, since products were sold there to buy return cargoes of molasses.

A smuggling trade from the French West Indies promptly began. New England shipmasters knew every half-hidden inlet and cove along the coast where a ship could enter and put a molasses cargo ashore by night, and they knew how to elude British patrol vessels lurking off the coast to stop and search inbound American merchantmen. The merchant–shipowners aided them with instructions on concealing contraband cargo under a vessel's hatches, by falsifying cargo manifests and by bribing British tidesmen, or customs inspectors, not to see certain things when inspecting a vessel's holds. The British customs officials at New England seaports and the patrol vessels found themselves baffled.

Benedict Arnold was one of the smugglers. He did a great

deal of business with the West Indies, and molasses was the principal return cargo aboard his ships. He owned three small vessels, the *Fortune*, the *Charming Nancy* and the *Three Brothers*. Being a smuggler was no disgrace; the New England colonies were seething with anger against the British government and the detested Sugar Act.

Some New Englanders agreed that Britain had a right to a fair revenue from her American colonies, but at the seaports groups of indignant radicals who would eventually push America into the Revolution were fuming. Arnold was among the most active of these radicals in New Haven. He urged that, if necessary, force should be used to stop what the radicals felt was robbery and violation of their rights by the British government.

It was the *Fortune*, which had been involved in Arnold's duel in the Caribbean, that caused his new trouble. In January 1766 the *Fortune* put in to New Haven from the West Indies, presumably with contraband French molasses in her holds. One of the vessel's sailors, Peter Boles, approached Arnold with a demand for extra wages. Arnold smelled an attempt at blackmail and refused.

On January 29 Arnold learned that Boles had gone to the customs house on January 24 to tell the British authorities of Arnold's smuggling. The collector was away, but Boles, without revealing what he knew, asked an assistant what share of a seized ship's cargo an informer would get. The official could not tell him, and Boles decided to wait for the collector's return.

Arnold took quick action. He went to the tavern where Boles was staying and, as he later described it, "gave him a little chastisement." Boles then left New Haven temporarily

but soon returned to try to see the collector. This was reported to Arnold, who hurried back to the tavern, found
Boles and made him sign a written statement. In it the sailor
declared that, instigated by the devil, he had attempted to
inform on Arnold, that he justly deserved hanging, that he
would never again inform on anyone in the colony and that
he would leave New Haven at once and never come back.

Boles signed but was not intimidated. He took refuge in the
tavern, resolved to carry out his plan. A few hours later
Arnold heard a commotion in the street. A group of his sailors
(with few exceptions his sailors and soldiers were always
staunchly loyal to Arnold) had gathered outside Boles's
retreat. Arnold took charge and they broke into the tavern,
mauled Boles, dragged him to the town green, where they
tied him to the public whipping post and gave him forty
lashes with "a small cord," and then ran him out of town.

Arnold was rid of Boles, but a group in New Haven who
supported Britain's policies decided to give the town's mob
of radicals a lesson. A justice of the peace ordered Arnold
and nine others bound over for trial for the attack on Boles.
The next day a mob roamed the New Haven streets, hanging
and burning dummies representing the conservatives who had
caused the arrests. At the trial Arnold was found guilty and
fined fifty shillings.

Meanwhile, as a successful merchant, he was living beyond
his means. Soon, because of a financial problem that beset the
colonies in 1767, Arnold, as well as other merchants and
tradesmen, was desperate for cash. The reason was a scarcity
of "hard money"—gold and silver coins, also known as
specie.

Arnold never had any scruples about making money in ways that were questionable if not illegal. He went into a rather shady deal involving foreign exchange, hoping to make a profit, but he did not succeed. Although in debt, he nevertheless managed to continue his trading and in time accumulated enough money and credit to live in higher style than ever.

THREE

A Revolutionary Stew Boils Over

In spite of his debts, Arnold was considered one of New Haven's prosperous merchants and was socially acceptable to most of the "better people." Not even his reputation as a radical affected his standing, and when he was received as a member of the Masonic Lodge of New Haven, it was a ticket of admission to the best social circles. He craved this recognition almost as much as money.

He had ample qualifications for social success. In addition to being considered a successful businessman, Arnold rode a horse with style and grace, skated expertly, was a crack shot with a pistol and dressed in the height of fashion. As a bachelor he was in great demand at routs, as evening social affairs were called, and the young women of New Haven sighed hopefully when he danced with them.

Among the prominent families in New Haven were the Mansfields. Samuel Mansfield was a well-to-do merchant and high sheriff of New Haven County. His daughter, Margaret, had a long string of suitors for her hand. But when Benedict Arnold, three years older than she, met and fell in love with her, he tumbled the other suitors aside like so many bowling pins. Margaret (he called her Peggy) was swept off her feet. On February 22, 1767, the two were married.

Arnold showed his passionate love for Peggy by showering her with luxuries he could not afford. He worked harder than ever to expand his trading business, while both Peggy and Hannah tended the New Haven drugstore. He now owned four ships and kept them busy in the West Indies trade, although he received a setback when the *Sally* was temporarily seized because of money he owed. One vessel, a sloop, traded between Quebec and the West Indian island of Barbados. Arnold went to Quebec often to trade horses and amassed a knowledge of the fortress-city on its towering rock above the St. Lawrence River that would be invaluable to him later. Invaluable, too, was the acquaintance with the area around Lake Champlain extending northward to Montreal that he gained during his rovings in search of products for export.

Peggy had to have a house suitable to her high social standing. Arnold bought property on Water Street in New Haven in 1770 and began building a mansion. The elegant two-story house, faced with white clapboards, was completed in 1771. It had two chimneys, a portico with pillars in the front and a marble fireplace on the ground floor, where the rooms were beautifully paneled. On the second floor each bedroom had a fireplace and was handsomely furnished. In cellars under the chimneys, fine wines were stored.

The grounds were equally magnificent. In front of the house was a white picket fence; in the rear were stables, a coach house and gardens with graveled walks. On the rest of the three-acre property stood maples, elms and fruit trees.

In the near distance were Arnold's wharves and a fine view
of Long Island Sound. It was a house of which Benedict and
Peggy Arnold could be proud, one of the best in all New
Haven.

Yet envious people were spreading malicious tales about
Arnold. A Captain Brookman told venomous stories about
Arnold's behavior during his voyages to the West Indies, and
Arnold challenged him to a duel. Brookman had his choice
of weapons and, being a skilled fencer, selected swords. But
he had not reckoned with Arnold's strength and dexterity and
was defeated.

Benedict and Peggy Arnold's first son, the sixth Benedict,
was born in 1768, and their second child, Richard, the following year, before they moved into the new house. A third son,
Henry, was born in 1772.

Arnold had to be away a great deal, of course, but he
looked eagerly for word from Peggy when some ship arrived
in a port where his vessel lay. Peggy was a loving wife but
no letter writer; even though Arnold wrote constantly, she
never became a good correspondent, causing him endless
worry and disappointment.

The days of the late 1760s and early 1770s were critical
ones for the American colonies. The British, by their continued efforts to obtain revenue from America, were stirring
up rebellion. In 1765, when the Stamp Act required tax
stamps on every sort of document in the colonies, there were
uprisings all over America; British-appointed stamp distribu-
tors were forced to resign, and people refused to buy the
stamps. The Stamp Act was repealed by Parliament, only to
be replaced by the Townshend Acts of 1767, placing import
taxes on glass, lead, paints and tea. These laws, too, caused

resistance by the colonies. In 1770 in Boston, where the strongest opposition to Britain was centered, a mob tormenting a British sentry caused a detachment of redcoats sent to his aid to fire on the rioters, killing five Americans. This incident came close to starting the American Revolution then and there. Three years later, in 1773, the famous Boston Tea Party took place when radicals dumped three cargoes of British tea into Boston harbor in protest against the tax that Parliament had imposed on tea. Britain's retaliation—closing the port of Boston—brought America to the very threshold of war.

Arnold was in the thick of the opposition to Britain in New Haven. The Sons of Liberty, so active in stirring up violence against Britain, was a secret organization, and only the names of a few leaders such as the great Samuel Adams are known. Yet there is no reason to doubt that Arnold was a member and took part in the activities against what was considered British tyranny.

In 1774, when Britain closed the port of Boston, patriots all over the American colonies began organizing companies of militia. In New Haven sixty-five men who called themselves "gentlemen of influence and high respectability" formed a military company. Each member was required to equip himself with arms and a uniform, and they hired an instructor to drill and prepare them to fight. Arnold was one of the original members.

His military career proves beyond doubt that he was a great fighter and leader, but there is question about his reasons for putting aside his money-making trade to become a Revolutionary officer. Was it true patriotism? Was it resentment against the British for interfering with his molasses-smuggling trade? Or was it his driving urge to win glory for himself?

Whatever his reasons, Arnold had qualities of leadership that brought him to command soon after the New Haven company was formed. In March 1775 the Connecticut General Assembly granted the group a charter as the "Governor's Second Company of Guards" and the right to select its own officers. The members chose Arnold as their captain.

After "the shot heard round the world" was fired at Lexington on April 19, 1775, to start the Revolution, word of it took two days to reach New Haven. On April 21 a rider galloped into town with the news.

A town meeting was immediately held in the "Middle Brick" church. The conservative element that opposed outright war was strong in New Haven, yet Roger Sherman, a moderate radical, was elected chairman of the meeting. Nevertheless, the conservatives were able to carry a motion not to send armed aid to the rebels outside Boston.

As far as Arnold was concerned, they had wasted their time. The moment the news of Lexington and Concord arrived, he had called out his company. About fifty turned up to hear Arnold propose that they march the next day for Cambridge, the rebels' headquarters outside Boston. The rest enthusiastically agreed. The company's ranks were increased by several Yale students who asked to join the company and were accepted.

It was no easy matter for Arnold to drop his trading ventures, place the drugstore in the hands of Hannah and Peggy and abruptly leave his family, but he did not hesitate. His wife, sister and the three small boys all went to see him off the next morning.

The Governor's Second Company of Guards, clad in scarlet uniforms, was drawn up in ranks on the green. Arnold was arrayed in the splendor of a scarlet coat trimmed with silver-coated buttons and buff-colored lapels, collar, cuffs and facings, a ruffled shirt, white waistcoat and breeches and black leggings.

A large crowd of New Haven citizens had gathered to watch. Arnold gave the onlookers a fine show when he paraded the Guards and inspected them to see that every man was properly equipped and armed.

One important thing was missing—ammunition. It was stored in the town powder house under the jurisdiction of the selectmen who governed New Haven. At that moment they were holding a meeting in a nearby tavern to discuss Arnold's defiance of the decision not to send troops to Cambridge.

While the Reverend Jonathan Edwards addressed the Guards and asked God's blessing on them, Arnold sent a request for powder and ball to the selectmen. They returned a blunt refusal.

Arnold bristled. He ordered his company to march to the tavern and drew them up in front of it. Then he sent in another message: deliver the key to the powder house to him within five minutes or he would order the door broken down.

Among the selectmen was an influential man, David Wooster. Although he was a conservative, he would soon offer his services to his country, become a somewhat undistinguished major general and later give his life for America. The selectmen sent him out to reason with Arnold.

Wooster did not try to give Arnold orders, for he knew

the Guards' commander was a purposeful man. Instead he urged him to dismiss the company and wait for official orders to march.

Arnold rasped out his reply: "None but God Almighty shall prevent me from marching!"

Wooster went back into the tavern and told the selectmen that Arnold was determined to have the ammunition. Some of them wanted to defy the Guards' commander, but they thought better of it and gave Arnold the key. Soon afterward the company was in marching order on the green again behind its resplendent flag with the Connecticut colony's motto, *Qui transtulit sustinet* ("He Who brought us here supports us"), emblazoned on it in gold. To the shrilling of fifes and the roll of drums, the company marched off.

It took them about a week to reach Cambridge, with a day of rest on the Sabbath. During the march every man, including Arnold, signed a pledge to avoid drunkenness, gambling and all other vices, and to obey their officers, who were not to enforce orders by blows. They agreed that any member of the company who persisted in violating these promises should be sent home.

Men were flooding into the American camp that encircled the narrow neck of land (later expanded by filling to form the city's Back Bay section) that at that time widened into the peninsula of Boston, but the smart appearance of Arnold's company got them special treatment. They were billeted in the fine mansion formerly occupied by royal Lieutenant Governor Thomas Oliver, who had fled to the safety of Boston. While they were there, a British officer, wounded and captured during the British expedition to Concord on April 19, died. Arnold's company was chosen to deliver the body to the commander in chief of the British troops in Boston, General Thomas Gage. The officer Gage delegated to receive the body expressed his amazement to see an American company who looked like soldiers.

He had good reason. British General "Gentleman Johnny" Burgoyne described what passed for the American army at that time as "a rabble in arms." A great many of the soldiers were dirty, unkempt, thieving, drunken men who shirked their duties. They obeyed the orders of their officers only when they felt like it. Most, good and bad, had come with their own muskets, if they had them. There was a critical shortage of powder, ball and, most of all, cannon.

Arnold's company was one of the few in uniform. Most of the others wore their farmer's, fisherman's or tradesman's clothes. And like Colonel Nathanael Greene, whose Rhode Island regiment was well clothed, equipped and disciplined, Arnold saw to it that his men kept their quarters and themselves neat and lived up to the agreement they had signed.

Arnold was not long at Cambridge. After observing the state of the "rabble in arms," he saw that the men must be better equipped, armed and trained if they were to have any chance of driving the British out of Boston. There was a very real possibility that the enemy would sally from the town and wipe the Americans out. Above all, cannon were needed to fortify the hills surrounding the land side of Boston, and a plan to get them was already buzzing in Arnold's mind.

During the march to Cambridge, Arnold had met and talked with Colonel Samuel H. Parsons, returning from the American camp to obtain badly needed recruits. Parsons had spoken of the desperate need for cannon.

Having come to know the Lake Champlain area while he

was trading in Canada, Arnold may have had a chance to observe British-held Fort Ticonderoga himself or he may have heard trappers and woods-rangers speak of its condition.

To most people in the American colonies, "Ticonderoga" meant an impregnable fortress. In 1758 General James Abercrombie's army had attempted to storm the fort, then held by the French and called Fort Carillon, and been repulsed in a bloody, devastating defeat. It had only been taken by Amherst in 1760 because the French had abandoned it. Its new name of Ticonderoga, in the minds of those who remembered Abercrombie's catastrophe, was an ugly word.

But Benedict Arnold knew that the British had neglected Ticonderoga, that it was beginning to crumble to ruin and was poorly and lightly garrisoned. And it had plenty of big cannon. Its capture would supply the heavy guns needed by the Americans outside Boston and would raise the morale of the colonists.

Action had to be taken swiftly, before the British got around to strengthening and reinforcing the fort. Arnold drew up a plan for an assault on Ticonderoga and presented it to the Massachusetts Committee of Safety, which was more or less in charge of American activities around Boston. He fumed as the committee, like so many others past and present, shilly-shallied, unable to make up its mind.

At last the great patriot Dr. Joseph Warren, soon to be killed at Bunker Hill, stirred the committee to action. It appointed Arnold a colonel and empowered him to raise four hundred men in western New England and assault the fortress. He was given arms and ammunition, ten horses and £100 in hard money. It was little enough money for an expedition of that size and importance, but this did not deter Arnold. At last he had his chance to show what a military genius could do. Leaving his company with the second in command, he started immediately for Stockbridge, in far western Massachusetts.

FOUR

The Man Who
Faced Arnold Down

Riding as fast as possible for Stockbridge, Arnold had no idea that several other men were also making plans for an assault on Ticonderoga. Colonel Parsons, whom Arnold and his company had met on their way to Cambridge, also was aware of the American army's need for cannon.

When Parsons reached Hartford, he had Ticonderoga on his mind and discussed the idea with some of the town's prominent men. They agreed that the capture of Ticonderoga was highly desirable but it must be done quickly. Taking the subject up with the Connecticut General Assembly would cause delay. They decided to go ahead and try to raise men, money and supplies themselves.

Meanwhile another man had been thinking of Ticonderoga. He was a giant with a voice to rival the rolling thunder of storms over the peaks of the Green Mountains in the New Hampshire Grants, today's Vermont. His speech was laced with profanity and quotations from the Old Testament that spoke of vengeance and hell fire.

The giant, Ethan Allen, had moved from Cornwall, Connecticut, to live on the Grants at Bennington. The settlers there had come from western Massachusetts and Connecticut after the French and Indian War and bought titles to their land from the colony of New Hampshire. The New York colony also laid claim to the Grants. When land speculators from New York tried to force out holders of New Hampshire titles, Ethan Allen started a "war" with the "Yorkers."

He organized the Green Mountain Boys, a group of tough, hard-drinking, leathery and red-necked farmers. They scared the wits out of New York speculators, sheriffs and their posses, who were armed with writs of ejectment to oust the New Hampshire title holders. The Green Mountain Boys threatened, manhandled and whipped the interlopers and sub-jected them to public scorn and derision. Allen once captured two Yorkers, held them prisoners overnight in separate places and in the early dawn took each one out in turn to view, at a distance, a dummy suspended by a rope from the limb of a tree. Allen told each that although he had hanged his com-panion, he was letting him go on condition that he never show his face on the Grants again. Neither did, but their surprise and discomfiture can be imagined when they met each other several weeks later on a street in Albany.

Once news of the war against Britain trickled over the mountain trails of the Grants, Allen forgot about fighting the Yorkers. He had already had a meeting early in 1775 with John Brown of Pittsfield in western Massachusetts. The rebel Committee of Correspondence in Boston had sent Brown to Canada to see how many French Canadians would join America in the coming war against their old enemies, the British. Brown had returned convinced that Britain would launch an invasion of the colonies from Canada by way of

Lake Champlain. When he reached the New Hampshire Grants, he met with Allen and other leaders of the Green Mountain Boys.

The conference was undoubtedly held at the Catamount Tavern in Bennington, headquarters for Allen and his men. In the tavern yard stood a tall pole. At its top was mounted a stuffed catamount, facing westward toward New York, its teeth bared as if snarling ferociously at the Yorker enemy. Inside the spacious tavern was a special chamber marked "Counsil Room," set aside for the Green Mountain Boys' meetings.

Since the idea of stopping a British invasion from Canada by capturing Ticonderoga, which guarded the invasion route (the only way was by water up Lake Champlain), was presumably already in Allen's mind, he probably suggested it to John Brown. It is definitely known that after the conference Brown sent a secret dispatch to Sam Adams in Boston saying that the Green Mountain Boys were ready to seize Ticonderoga.

Allen had five brothers, all residents of the New Hampshire Grants. In Hartford, while leaders in the Connecticut General Assembly were discussing the proposed expedition with Colonel Parsons, Allen's brother Heman was in town; like Ethan, Heman made frequent business trips back to Connecticut. It was known in Hartford that Ethan was ready to lead an attack on Ticonderoga. The Hartford group asked Heman Allen to meet with them.

When Heman galloped back north, he carried a commission for Ethan to march against Ticonderoga and a promise that money and additional troops would be sent along to aid the Green Mountain Boys. The Hartford group then raised

£300, which was taken north by a company of about twenty volunteers who were joined on the way by about forty-nine others and two officers, including John Brown.

Meanwhile, in Stockbridge, Arnold had been raising his own force. When he learned that Allen was about to march for Ticonderoga, he left an officer in Stockbridge to continue recruiting and rode north in a towering rage. Arnold was going to have a little talk with this bumpkin, Allen, and make it clear that any force that assaulted Ticonderoga would be commanded by himself, not Allen.

Benedict Arnold collided with Ethan Allen on May 9, 1775, at Zadock Remington's tavern in Castleton, on the Grants, where the Green Mountain Boys had assembled. The argument that took place in the taproom almost blew the roof off the tavern.

Both men were attired splendidly, Arnold in his scarlet and buff and Allen in a uniform he had created himself. According to tradition, his coat was forest green, profusely ornamented with gold, including its buttons, and topped by enormous epaulettes.

Arnold arrogantly told Allen that *he*, Benedict Arnold, by authority of the Massachusetts Committee of Safety, was the supreme commander of the expedition. Allen, in a voice like a salvo of cannon, larded with sizzling oaths, told Arnold to get back where he came from, fast, and never return to the New Hampshire Grants.

It was the oft-repeated case of the immovable object meeting the irresistible force. But for the presence of the Green Mountain Boys in the tavern yard, the argument might have ended in a duel whose outcome, despite Arnold's small size, would have been unpredictable. Allen's men, hearing the tempest inside, discussed what they should do with this macaroni (dandy) in a redcoat's uniform who thought he could take the command away from "old Ethan." (Allen was only thirty-three years old but they spoke with affection.) Some favored seizing Arnold and dunking him in a nearby stream to cool him off. At length, however, they crowded into the tavern and told Arnold in menacing and profane language that unless old Ethan led them against Ticonderoga they would all go home. Let Arnold march alone and capture the fortress.

There was nothing Arnold could do but yield. For the first and probably the only time in his life he had been faced down by a rival. Nevertheless, when the Green Mountain Boys marched, Arnold was right beside Allen at the head of the straggling column. He issued no orders, however, for he knew they would not be obeyed.

An advance guard, sent ahead to Hand's Cove on the Grants side of Lake Champlain across from Ticonderoga, failed to round up more than a few canoes to ferry across the two hundred-odd men who gathered there that night of May 9. Another search turned up two good-sized scows, but only about eighty-five men, with Arnold squeezed in among them, were immediately able to cross the narrow stretch of water in the fast-approaching dawn.

In the gray light they surprised a lone sentry who, when his musket misfired, yelled an alarm as he scrambled up from a wicket gate in the walls to the ramparts. Allen, Arnold and the rest of the party followed and easily captured Ticonderoga's commander, Captain William Delaplace; his only other officer, a lieutenant; forty-three redcoats, some of them decrepit; and the fortress itself.

Arnold, glowering and disconsolate, watched the celebration while the Green Mountain Boys, having discovered the fort's stock of liquor, "tossed about the flowing bowl," as Allen later described it. Arnold felt he had been shamefully robbed of a chance for fame.

In fact, more humiliation lay just ahead. Arnold was disgusted with the lack of discipline among the victorious Green Mountain Boys and again demanded that Allen yield the command. But by that time the additional Connecticut force had arrived, and its leader, Captain Edward Mott, directed Allen to remain in command. An account of the dispute was sent to the Massachusetts Committee of Safety.

Nevertheless, Arnold had revenge. Ethan Allen was now determined to travel down the Richelieu River from its outlet at the north end of Lake Champlain and capture Montreal, which was as poorly defended by the British as it had been by the French in 1760. He would then continue down the St. Lawrence River and take Quebec, completing the American conquest of Canada.

An obstacle was St. Johns, a post on the Richelieu about twenty miles north of Champlain's outlet. However, the British defenses there were weak, and Allen decided to advance against St. Johns. Since the attack had to be made by water, Arnold, with his long experience at sea, was given command of the expedition.

He grabbed a schooner that the Americans had captured at Skenesboro, near the south end of the lake, renamed her the *Liberty* and put thirty-five of his newly arrived Massachusetts men aboard. Allen and ninety-six Green Mountain Boys followed in slow, clumsy, flat-bottomed bateaux. The *Liberty* quickly outdistanced the bateaux, which had to depend upon oars in addition to their sails. But when the wind dropped to a dead calm the bateaux began to overhaul the *Liberty*. Arnold was too clever to lose the lead, however. He transferred his men to the schooner's small boats and rowed like mad for St. Johns, thirty miles away. Soon the unwieldy bateaux dropped astern and out of sight.

Arnold caught the small, weak post at St. Johns completely by surprise. Its garrison of fourteen redcoats, commanded by a sergeant, surrendered at once. Arnold burned the five bateaux that were there, captured a fair-sized enemy sloop, put some of his men aboard and renamed her the *Enterprise*.

Just then word reached him that two hundred British troops were on their way to St. Johns. He was too good a military man to trade bullets with a force of that size and headed back toward Lake Champlain. On the way he met Allen's slow-moving bateaux.

Arnold could now afford to be magnanimous. He ordered a salute to Allen fired and invited him aboard the sloop. Allen swallowed his own humiliation and came over for a few toasts to the Continental Congress. But when Arnold warned him about the two hundred British approaching St. Johns, Allen boastfully announced that he would take the place anyhow and move on to Montreal.

For all the fame of his triumph at Ticonderoga, Allen was no great general or strategist. He ran into a hornets' nest when he allowed his tired men to sleep on the opposite side of the river from St. Johns. They were awakened in the morning by a storm of cannon balls from the newly arrived British detachment's artillery across the river and were lucky to escape with their lives in the bateaux.

Back at Ticonderoga, Arnold and Allen were soon at each other's throats again. Both were still determined to capture Montreal. Reinforcements kept arriving for Arnold's force, while many of the Green Mountain Boys returned to their farms on the Grants. Arnold soon seized command.

There was a great deal of maneuvering by both men after that. Arnold wrote to the newly created Massachusetts Provincial Congress, hoping it would appoint him to command a Canadian invasion. With the same idea, Allen wrote to the Continental Congress in Philadelphia. As the bad feeling between the two men continued, Arnold moved his headquarters a little north to the American defense post at Crown Point.

Receiving no reply to his first letter, Arnold wrote two more to the Massachusetts Provincial Congress requesting that he be relieved of his duties at Ticonderoga and Crown Point. What he probably wanted was an authoritative expression of confidence in him. Finally he got it in a letter expressing full satisfaction with all he had done and the Congress's wish that he continue in command.

This was pleasing, but Arnold had enemies in Massachusetts. A committee from there arrived suddenly to investigate him. With them was Colonel Benjamin Hinman of Connecticut, who took over the command with the committee's backing. Arnold, beside himself with rage over this double cross by the Massachusetts Provincial Congress, resigned.

~~If~~ Arnold had ~~been~~ given command of a strong force to move on practically defenseless Montreal, he ~~almost~~ certainly would have captured it. Instead, Ethan Allen, sent into Canada to recruit volunteers, ~~took~~ the conquest of Montreal into his own hands, without authority from any superior. His assault on the city failed so miserably that the weak British force repulsed his volunteers and captured him. He spent nearly all the rest of the Revolution as a prisoner of war.

Meanwhile Arnold was asked to come to the Albany head-quarters of General Philip Schuyler, in command of the newly created Northern Continental Army. There he began drawing up a detailed report for the Continental Congress on the state of the defenses and troops at Ticonderoga, Crown Point and, to the south of them, Fort George.

Arnold was in a bad humor, feeling that the Massachusetts Congress, by compelling him to account for all public money he had spent in the Champlain area, had put a stain on his honor. (Actually, he had paid £2,500 of his own money for provisions and clothing for the troops.) An attack of gout further aggravated his ill temper.

Then came the worst blow. While he was in Albany, word reached Arnold that his beloved Peggy, only thirty-three years old, had died. He abandoned his report and, over-whelmed with grief, rode to his wife's grave and his three motherless sons in New Haven.

FIVE

The March to Quebec

Arnold's sister, Hannah, went took over the care of his three boys, then seven, six and three years old. Until they were grown up, she had full charge of them and remained dedicated to their welfare and that of her brother almost to the end of her life. Aside from his two wives, Hannah was the only really close friend Arnold ever had.

For a time Arnold stayed in New Haven. He looked after his neglected trading affairs until he was bedridden by a severe attack of gout. When he had recovered sufficiently and could ride a horse, he once again left Hannah in charge of his business affairs and departed for Cambridge. In his absence, Hannah efficiently negotiated an important trading venture in which Arnold was to ship sixty thousand staves, heads and hoops for hogsheads to the West Indies. With the help of a New Haven businessman, Silas Deane, who was later to become famous as a diplomat seeking French aid for the embattled colonies, the deal appears to have been accomplished.

Arnold received shabby treatment in Cambridge, where he made a report to the Massachusetts Provincial Congress. The Congress was still investigating his financial dealings during and following the Ticonderoga expedition. They appointed a

committee to ferret out any unauthorized expenditures of the
public money, despite Arnold's counterclaim that the Congress owed him money. Considerably later, most of the money
found due him was paid and sent to Hannah.

The idea of an expedition against Quebec was in the minds
of several men, but it was Arnold who worked out a detailed
plan for one starting from Cambridge. In Albany General
Schuyler was already busy with plans for the conquest of
Canada by way of Lake Champlain, taking St. Johns, then
Montreal, and continuing on to Quebec. The Cambridge
expedition would be invaluable to him. If it reached Quebec
first, it might well be able to capture the city itself, since
Governor Sir Guy Carleton, commanding general of the
British forces in Canada, would have had to take most of his
army to meet Schuyler's expected advance at Montreal, leaving the fortress on the Rock weakly defended. Or the Cambridge expedition might force Carleton to send some of his
troops back to Quebec. In any event, if Schuyler captured
Montreal and moved down the St. Lawrence, he would have
additional Americans to complete his conquest.

Arnold was determined to see that the Cambridge expedition was carried out, with himself in supreme command.
General George Washington had arrived in Cambridge and
Arnold submitted his plan directly to the commander in
chief.

Arnold ~~didn't have~~ Had much to work on. The part of Maine
an expedition must penetrate to reach the province of Quebec
was largely unknown wilderness. In 1761, after the British
conquest of Canada, General James Murray had sent an
engineer, Lieutenant John Montresor, to explore the region.
Arnold obtained Montresor's report and a map he had drawn.

This at least enabled him to plan a route, largely by water, that would reach the Chaudière River, flowing northward through Quebec and into the St. Lawrence near the city on the Rock. What Montresor failed to show were all the perils of the journey.

In Cambridge the greatest obstacle Arnold had to face was time. If the expedition was to succeed, it had to start early enough to avoid the cold and the deep snows of winter and also to be sure of meeting Schuyler outside the city. Washington was cautious, but the two-pronged drive on Quebec was so important that he offered the command to Arnold, who accepted and plunged into preparations immediately.

On August 21, on behalf of the commander in chief, Arnold wrote to Reuben Colburn, a boat builder on the Kennebec River in Maine, asking how soon two hundred light bateaux to carry six or eight men each and about a hundred pounds of cargo could be built and what they would cost. He also asked Colburn for all possible information about the route and if fresh beef could be obtained at the starting point.

Whose idea was it to use bateaux rather than canoes? It may have been Arnold's, Washington's or a joint decision. It was Washington who ordered them from Colburn at forty shillings apiece, to include four oars, two paddles and four setting poles to propel the boats in shallow water. But the commander in chief was depending on Arnold's plan.

If the decision was Arnold's, then the first and only mistake of his military career must be charged against him. He knew that even light bateaux were heavy and clumsy. Yet canoes were unstable craft, easily capsized in rough water or rapids, and many more than two hundred would have been needed because of their smaller capacity. Nevetherless, if Arnold had known what lay ahead of him, he probably would have used canoes.

Washington also ordered Colburn to "bespeak all the Pork and Flour you can from the Inhabitants upon the River Kennebeck" and to notify them that sixty barrels of beef would also be needed.

The expedition included two battalions of five companies each, a total of 742 officers and men, as well as Captain Daniel Morgan's company of Virginia riflemen and two companies of Pennsylvania riflemen, about 250 in all. With a surgeon and assistants, a chaplain and other commissioned and noncommissioned officers, the entire number was 1,051. This also included six volunteers not attached to any company, one of whom—Aaron Burr—was later to become famous. For the expedition's expenses, Arnold was supplied £1,000 specie— "hard money," or coin.

Marching overland in detachments from Cambridge, the entire expedition reached Newburyport by September 13. There eleven sloops and schooners took them by sea to the Kennebec's mouth and about twenty-five miles upriver to Gardiner.

Arnold, elegant in his scarlet and buff uniform, with a plumed cocked hat, went ashore to inspect the bateaux. To his dismay the two hundred hastily constructed craft were badly built and some were smaller than ordered. Seasoned timber had been eked out with green wood. But they proved satisfactory on the deep, wide and not-too-swift-flowing Kennebec at Gardiner.

They pushed on up to Fort Western (today Maine's capital, Augusta). Arnold sent two companies ahead in canoes.

One was to trace out the route to big Lake Megantic, across the Quebec border, from which the Chaudière flowed. Arnold suspected that Natanis and his Abnaki warriors were in the wilderness ahead, probably to spy on the expedition for the British. He ordered the second rifle company to hunt Natanis down and either capture or kill what the leader described as "that noted villain."

The main force was separated into four divisions. The first, Captain Morgan's sharp-shooting Virginians, was sent ahead to clear the trail over the carrying places around falls and rapids. Its most important task was to prepare a route over the Great Carrying Place between the upper Kennebec and the Dead River.

Morgan was rivaled only by Arnold as a fighting man. His Virginians would have marched through hell at his command. He was a tower of strength to Arnold throughout Arnold's military career. Fighting until ill health forced him to retire, Morgan was one of the Revolution's greatest heroes.

The second division of three companies, under Lieutenant Christopher Greene, left the next day. Twenty-four hours later the third division of four companies, led by Major Return Jonathan Meigs, departed, followed the next day by the fourth division, commanded by Lieutenant Colonel Roger Enos. Arnold then set out in a canoe for the head of the column.

Trouble that would not end until the force approached Quebec began a half mile above Fort Western. The boats were blocked by impassable rapids. Farmers of the region hauled the bateaux on wagons and sleds until they could be launched again, but even then the current was so swift that it took the oarsmen and polers two days to reach the abandoned military post of Fort Halifax, eighteen miles above. By that time the green wood in the bateaux had swelled, making them leaky, and many had been gashed by sharp rocks in shallow rapids. It was necessary to beach the boats and put three companies to work caulking the leaks.

Even more serious was the destruction of Dr. Isaac Senter's bateau in the rapids and the loss of his store of medicines. He told of it in his diary, which was one of a number kept by the officers and men, including Arnold.

Just above Fort Halifax the expedition was stopped again, this time by Taconic Falls. Most of the supplies in the bateaux had to be unloaded, slung on poles and laboriously carried overland. Each four-hundred-pound bateau was transported on the shoulders of four men. Altogether, they wrestled a weight of about a hundred tons around the falls. It was the first of many portages.

Beyond was a stretch of extremely dangerous rapids. The oarsmen continually had to jump overboard, up to their waists and sometimes chins in icy water, to push the bateaux upstream. Approaching Skowhegan, they passed through a gorge about twenty-five feet wide and around a sharp turn, with the narrowed river racing at great speed. At the head of the gorge were more falls, divided by a narrow cleft in the middle, through which the boats and their loads had to be carried. Then they pushed through five miles of rapids and small waterfalls.

After they passed Skowhegan, the canyonlike walls closed in again through the torrent of Bombazee Rips. Then came the hardest carry yet, a mile and a half around the three great cataracts of Norridgewock Falls. Some inhabitants of this region hauled the supplies in ox carts while the men staggered over the portage with the boats on their shoulders. Above Norridgewock all habitation ceased; beyond was only trackless wilderness.

The expedition camped overnight at a lodge just above the falls. The journey to Quebec had no more than begun, but already most of the boats were little more than wrecks, some stove to pieces by the rocks. The water in them had washed the salt out of the dried, salted codfish that had been loaded loose in the bateaux, and it had spoiled. So had the salt beef. Casks of bread and dried peas had burst as they soaked up water.

Arnold had ordered provisions to last forty-five days for a journey he estimated at 180 miles (it was more) and expected to cover in twenty days. They were now, on October 2, eight days out of Gardiner, having moved less than a quarter of the distance to Quebec, with far worse going ahead. Their food supply was reduced to flour and pork.

It took them three days to do a makeshift job of repairing the boats. During this time the rear divisions of Meigs and Enos came up with the leading ones. It was October 9 before their baggage was carried around the falls and the expedition could proceed.

For the next two days the going was easier, with only one short portage around Carritunk Falls, but the weather was vile, with continual cold rain. Snow-capped mountains appeared on each side of the river.

On October 11 the expedition reached the Great Carrying Place between the Kennebec and the Dead River and began its most exhausting trial thus far. Daniel Morgan and his men and Lieutenant Colonel Greene's second division were already there. Arnold kept on the move backward and forward to see that all was as well as could be expected with the whole force.

Morgan's advance party had done what it could to improve the Great Carrying Place (four portages, with ponds between them), but the trail was still rough and the going bad. The first portage, over three miles long, ran through thick forest. Part of it was filled with bogs in which the men sank knee deep, and part with great ledges. Some of the men stumbled under the weight of the boats, while others carried pork strung on poles. It took seven or eight trips to get everything across. All the while, rain mixed with sleet was driving into the men's faces with gale force.

A bit of luck came to the expedition at the first pond. They were able to catch many fine salmon trout, and a moose was killed, giving the men a welcome change from baked flour-and-water cakes and pork and conserving the food supply. They crossed the pond, a mile and a quarter long, and found the second portage comparatively easy and short. But the water in the second pond, two and a half miles long, was yellow and stagnant. Some of the thirsty, exhausted men drank it and became so sick that, after crossing, it was necessary to build a crude hospital, which was promptly filled. Some of the men were severely ill.

During this terrible crossing of the Great Carrying Place, the parties Arnold had sent ahead, one to reconnoiter the Dead River and the other as far as the Chaudière, returned. The latter had gotten through but came close to never returning. The leader, Captain Archibald Steele, and seven riflemen had started back through a rainstorm that lasted a day and a half. Their provisions ran out, but they shot a duck, picked its bones clean, eating even its head and feet, and pushed on fifty miles in their two canoes. When a submerged snag ripped one craft's ribs from stem to stern, they managed to patch it up, only to have a second snag break it in half five hundred yards farther on. Somehow they put it back together.

Hope revived among Steele's party when one of them shot a moose, but when they ate it, all became sick. According to the journal kept by one of the men, John Joseph Henry, this was caused by a lack of salt for curing the meat. Five men were so desperately ill that Lieutenant Steele and the other two had to abandon them and push on for help. The five were finally found by some of Morgan's men. By then they were gaunt bags of skin and bone, barely able to stumble on.

Arnold sent advance parties ahead again, with twenty ax men, to clear the other portages. The expedition followed, leaving eight or ten men, seriously ill with dysentery, in the hospital. Dr. Senter wrote that the arms and legs of some were swollen to such enormous size that the patients could not move them.

Arnold described the third portage as "long and very bad." The boats were then rowed three miles across the pond to its end. The fourth and last portage was nearly three miles long. At first the trail was fairly good; then it plunged into boggy grassland with ooze six or eight inches deep. They camped before wading through it the next morning.

The two leading divisions reached the Dead River on October 13, and the rest three days later. Its grisly name appeared justified at first, for the water was black, deep and deceptively smooth. Actually the current was so swift that the oarsmen made no headway rowing against it and had to drag the boats along by pulling on branches along the steep banks.

The Dead River did come close to being the death of them all. On the first day, while the river writhed like a stricken snake and it seemed they were putting no distance behind them, an even more discouraging discovery was made. The food supply of the leading division was nearly exhausted.

Worse was yet to come. For three days, beginning October 19, rain fell steadily. By October 21 it was torrential, with gale-force winds. Great trees crashed into the river, blocking all passage. The drenched force had to camp. There were few tents, and the hemlock shelters the men put up offered little protection. During the night the river overflowed its banks, which were eight or ten feet high. Precious barrels of pork were swept away as bateaux filled and sank. The whole camp was driven up a hill to escape drowning.

The rain stopped about midnight and by morning a cold wind was blowing. The men, hungry, soaked and chilled, saw a terrifying sight. The night before, the river had been sixty yards wide; now it was two hundred, with its overflow covering the entire countryside. A lake four feet deep lay where a campfire had burned the previous evening.

The strongest of the boatmen managed to take Captain Morgan and his advance party up the river. The rest spent the day drying themselves and their baggage. Late in the afternoon Major Meigs's third division came up and joined them.

When the force pushed on the next day, most had to march overland. They took long detours around the flooded river valley. One detachment followed a tributary stream, and men had to be landed from the boats to find them.

On that dreadful day the worst disaster up to that time befell them. As they approached another carrying place, the current capsized seven bateaux loaded with practically all the remaining provisions, which were lost. With that, Arnold called a council of war.

There is nothing in his journal to indicate that at any time during the expedition he thought of giving up. The diary is a calm, matter-of-fact record of details, without a single word of complaint or despair. But he felt it was only fair to get the opinions of his officers about what should be done.

They might have voted to turn back but for the inspiration Arnold's determination gave them. The decision was to continue. However, twenty-six men whose condition made it impossible to go on were sent back to the hospital, followed soon afterward by forty-eight more.

Greene's division had come up with the rest but now fell behind because of lack of food. He had sent back to Enos's division asking for supplies, but Enos gave him only two barrels of flour, even though his division was better supplied than the rest.

The leading divisions pushed ahead, but Greene, waiting for the food, remained behind until Enos's division came up with him. These two, without authority, held their own council to decide what to do. Eleven officers took part and voted six to five to follow Arnold. When Greene asked that the available flour be shared with his division, Enos refused, saying he could not control his men. But he gave up two and a half barrels of flour, and Greene's division moved ahead.

Although Enos had voted to go on, he then led his division back to Fort Western, with enough flour to make the march comparatively easy, and on to Cambridge. Enos was later court-martialed for this act. He was acquitted, but public scorn soon forced him out of the army.

It was days before Arnold heard of Enos's retreat. Meanwhile he had sent Captain Oliver Hanchet of Major Meigs's division ahead with fifty men to the Chaudière settlements to obtain food. Arnold knew the expedition would reach its objective if the food could be brought back in time, but the chances were not good.

The little flour remaining was divided equally. The men also boiled a small supply of tallow candles to make a thin, greasy gruel. The force, reduced by Enos's desertion to less than seven hundred men, floundered on. Except for a partridge shot and devoured by a group of Captain Simeon Thayer's men of Greene's division, apparently no game was seen. Since there is no mention of fish, it appears that the means of catching them were lost with the other equipment.

At this time a sad incident occurred. Two women, wives of soldiers, were with the expedition. Both were magnificent, sharing the hardships without complaint. One of them, Mrs. Warner, learned during this worst period of the march that her husband had fallen, exhausted, to the rear. She went back to rescue him but was able to give him only what comfort she could in his dying moments.

After circling two waterfalls, the expedition left the Dead River and crossed several ponds. It rained or snowed continually. The land intervals were either ledge-ridden or marsh. Ahead lay the most fearful obstacle of all, a ridge of mountains called the Height of Land. If they could get over it, they would not be far from Lake Megantic, with its northern outlet the Chaudière.

This portage was four and a quarter miles long. With only a few bateaux left, there was, luckily, little to be carried. The force toiled painfully up the steep height and were so exhausted when they reached the top that they could barely totter down the other side to the Seven Mile Stream, leading to Megantic. They continued on for five miles before camping. The provisions were now down to five pints of flour and about two ounces of pork to each man.

The Seven Mile Stream was tricky, dividing into false stretches that ended in trackless swamps. Twice the expedition followed these false stretches; the second time the men became hopelessly lost seeking a way to the main stream. Still not in sight of it, they camped. Each man ate a quarter of a pint of flour, baked into a cake over the fire or simply mixed with water, and nibbled at his tiny ration of pork.

Next day they still floundered through bogs and deep forests until one company sighted the Seven Mile Stream and led the rest to it. Soon afterward a great huzza went up from the leading company. Ahead stretched Lake Megantic. It was October 27.

They reached the Chaudière the next morning. Arnold sent two officers and thirteen men in five bateaux and a canoe to bring back food from the first settlement.

The Chaudière is treacherous—swift, with many rapids, rocks and falls. Arnold and Morgan, with the remaining bateaux, started down and were caught in tumultuous rapids. Six of the boats were smashed and everything in them lost. One man was drowned. There was a bit of luck in it, however; just ahead was a concealed fall in which all those in the boats would have perished.

On November 1, with snow on the ground, the long, strung-out column moved on. The men on shore were so weak they could barely hobble. Few had any food at all. They boiled moccasins, shot pouches and worn-out leather breeches and chewed on them. In his diary Private George

Morison wrote: "No one can imagine, who has not experienced it, the sweetness of a roasted pouch to the famished appetite."

Captain William Goodrich had brought along his Newfoundland dog. What the big fellow subsisted on is not known, and by that time he must have been little more than skin and bones. Captain Goodrich was very fond of him, but his men killed the dog, eating every morsel of meat on the carcass and saving the bones for soup.

The next day was the crisis. Morison wrote: "Never perhaps was there a more forlorn set of human beings collected together ... shivering from head to foot, as hungry as wolves. ... It was a dispiriting, heart-rending sight to see these men ... struggling among rocks and in swamps and falling over logs ... falling down upon one another in the act of mutually assisting each other. . . . Many of the men began to fall behind. ... It was therefore given out ... by our officers for every man to shift for himself and save his own life if possible."

They had reached the end of their endurance when someone spied, like a mirage in the distance, cattle driven by horsemen coming toward them, followed by two canoe loads of mutton and flour. In moments the first animal was slaughtered and torn to pieces by the ravenous men, who swallowed the meat raw. More was quickly sent back to the long train of men behind them who had collapsed.

It was over. Many miles still lay between Arnold's expedition and Quebec, but they had won. Health and good spirits returned as Arnold stocked up with provisions along the way. Some men, however, stuffed themselves so voraciously that they were ill; three died from overeating after a period of near starvation.

At Sartigan they were joined by Natanis. He and his band of Abnakis had never lost sight of the expedition throughout the journey, but fear of capture or death had kept them from giving much assistance. Arnold changed his mind about the Indian chief when Natanis turned out to be friendly to the American cause. With his fifty braves he joined the expedition.

There have been few more grueling marches in military history. It is doubtful that most of the troops would have followed any other Revolutionary leader, except perhaps Daniel Morgan, through such a terrifying experience. If Arnold could have gotten to Enos's division before it turned back, it is likely that the men would have gone on. And he had brought the others through with an exceptionally small loss of life.

The first of Natanis's supposed predictions had been fulfilled. The wilderness had yielded to the Dark Eagle.

SIX

The Rock

The expedition's difficulties were by no means ended. Nevertheless, the force was now in better condition to move ahead. Provisions had revived the men to the rear. With their strength sufficiently recovered, these soldiers rejoined the others. Some, lying half dead in the snow, were brought forward on horses.

By November 10 the entire expedition had reached the mouth of the Chaudière. Arnold hoped to cross the St. Lawrence quickly, assault the fortress with its weak garrison and capture Quebec. Instead, everything went against him.

Indians friendly to the British had betrayed the Americans' approach to Lieutenant Governor Hector Cramahé, who was in command while Governor Carleton was in Montreal. Although he was no military expert, Cramahé had strengthened the city's defenses somewhat and collected all the boats that could be found along the St. Lawrence in the vicinity of Point Levi, directly opposite Quebec. A British frigate and a sloop-of-war lay off the city.

Worst of all, Arnold had dispatched a letter telling of his arrival to Brigadier General Richard Montgomery, who, because of the ill health of General Schuyler, had taken command of the American expedition approaching by way of Montreal. Arnold's dispatch had been intercepted by Scottish Lieutenant Colonel Allen Maclean, who had been driven out of Sorel, at the mouth of the Richelieu River, by the advancing Americans. Maclean had raised a force of 200 loyal Scots and was on a leisurely march. When he learned that Arnold was close to the city, he and his men pushed on with all possible speed.

Arnold might nevertheless have beaten Maclean to Quebec and assaulted the weakly defended city. He had managed to round up enough boats to make the crossing, but for three days a storm whipped the St. Lawrence into such a fury that no small boat could survive in it. Meanwhile Maclean and his men slipped into the city.

It was the night of November 13 before all but about 150 of Arnold's forces embarked, sneaked past the two British men-of-war in the darkness and landed above the city at Wolfe's Cove. The rest crossed during the following night. All scrambled up the same steep height that General James Wolfe's army had followed to the Plains of Abraham before meeting and defeating the Marquis de Montcalm in 1759.

Arnold now knew that an assault by his force alone would be foolhardy. Cramahé's garrison had numbered about 1,000, but it had been largely composed of inferior British and French Canadian militia and sailors from the warships. Maclean's 200 first-class fighting men had strengthened it. Arnold had only about 600 men, no artillery and no scaling ladders for getting over the city wall. While he did twice carry out the formality of sending demands for surrender toward the wall, cannon on the ramparts drove his messengers back. He would have to wait and hope that Montgomery's army would take Montreal and hasten on to Quebec.

To understand the difficulties the Americans faced in an assault, it is necessary to know what the fortress-city was like. Quebec stands on a high rock whose blunt point sticks out into the St. Lawrence. It was protected against attack from the plain behind it by a massive wall from which protruded six pointed bastions mounted with heavy cannon. Behind the three gates in the wall were small forts also mounted with guns. The St. Louis Gate, nearest the center of the wall, was the entrance for the road from Montreal, some 160 miles away.

At the southeastern end of the wall, steep, rocky Cape Diamond fell away in an almost sheer drop of over 300 feet. Between its foot and the St. Lawrence a narrow passage led to the Lower Town, a collection of a few houses, warehouses, wharves and a small church huddled on a little strip of level land at the foot of the Rock.

Running across the plain from Cape Diamond, the wall dipped down a fairly steep incline and curved around to end at the Palace Gate. From this gate a road climbed to the heart of Quebec, the Upper Town. Beyond the Palace Gate the walls of the Rock rose as nearly straight up as at Cape Diamond. Here another narrow passage, edging the curving shore of the St. Lawrence, also led to the Lower Town.

The Upper Town had to be taken before an American victory could be won. Perched on its highest point was a fortress, the Citadel. In the Upper Town were also the cathedral, churches and convents, the palace of the bishop, the governor's mansion, a college, the city hall, other public and government buildings and the dwellings of most of Quebec's residents.

There were three ways by which the Americans might get into the city. The first was an assault on the wall—by blasting holes in it, which would call for heavy artillery, or by climbing over it, which would require scaling ladders. If the wall could be penetrated or surmounted, this was the easiest way, since the attack could be launched from the level ground of the Plains of Abraham.

The second was an approach through the narrow way along the base of Cape Diamond to the Lower Town; the third, an approach by the equally constricted passage along the base of the Rock from beyond the Palace Gate to the Lower Town. Or a two-pronged attack might be made over both passages. In any case these attacks would have to surmount steep, well-defended Mountain Street, connecting the Lower Town with the Upper.

Since his force alone could not capture Quebec, Arnold set up a blockade of the city so that no food from its land side could come in. There was just a chance that the city might be starved out if a long siege was necessary.

Compared to what they had been through, Arnold's men were living in luxury. On the plain, about a mile and a half from the wall, stood a fine mansion owned by a British army officer that was now vacant. The Americans crammed themselves into the house and its numerous outbuildings. With plenty of food, warmth and time to recover fully from their march, the soldiers didn't mind if it took all winter to starve Quebec out.

These pleasant conditions were rudely interrupted when Arnold heard that Lieutenant Colonel Maclean planned to come out of the city with 800 troops and attack his force of about 600. There were also reports that a ship with 200 British reinforcements was coming up the river and that the British frigate *Lizard* had moved up the St. Lawrence so that men could be landed behind the Americans to cut off a possible retreat.

On the dark and bitter night of November 29, the Americans' misery returned when they had to make a secret twenty-mile march upriver to Pointe aux Trembles. The one thing the men still lacked was proper clothing, especially shoes, for most were barefoot and suffered agonies on the rough, frozen road. Nor did it help their spirits when, in the darkness, they made out an armed schooner slipping down the river toward Quebec. In it was Sir Guy Carleton, coming to take command of the city.

For two weeks Arnold's troops rested, being billeted in the cottages of French Canadians in Pointe aux Trembles. On December 2 loud cheers resounded through the village. A fleet carrying General Montgomery, 300 men, artillery, clothing and food was sighted coming down the river. The general's army had had no easy time in capturing the British defenses along the Richelieu River, but when it reached Montreal, the city had fallen quickly. Carleton had lost his army and practically all his fleet, but he himself had made a miraculous escape disguised as a countryman.

Montgomery had captured not only a large stock of supplies but enough British winter uniforms to equip his own and Arnold's forces. The uniforms included heavy white overcoats with cape-hoods and underjackets of the same material, as well as sealskin moccasins. Now the Americans were ready for Quebec.

Montgomery was a general everyone liked—a tall, slender, handsome man, mild and gentle yet resolute in purpose. He did not have Arnold's bold recklessness, but he was a good soldier.

On December 5 the combined army marched back to the Plains of Abraham. Arnold's force took quarters in the suburb of St. Roche on the far left, occupying part of the large General Hospital there. Arnold himself set up headquarters in Menut's Tavern, near Montgomery's headquarters and camp, facing the middle section of the wall.

Although Quebec was now blockaded again on the land side, Montgomery knew that a siege was out of the question. Schuyler wanted Quebec taken as soon as possible. Ordinarily a besieging army would advance by digging a series of parallel trenches (each one a little nearer its objective and reached by short connecting trenches) while its artillery weakened enemy defenses. But the deeply frozen ground could not be dug out. Moreover, the enlistments of Arnold's men would expire January 1, 1776, and after the ordeal of their march, followed by the blizzards, gales and rock-splitting cold of the Quebec winter, it was all too certain that they would go home then. An assault must be made before the year's end.

Montgomery had no more faith than Arnold in getting Quebec to surrender without a fight, but he too tried. Two messengers demanding surrender and pointing out the weakness of Carleton's troops were repulsed. Arrows carrying a similar message were sent whizzing over the wall, but without effect.

Meanwhile the Americans tried to build emplacements for their artillery. Ordinarily, they would have used platforms of earth, but since digging was impossible, they froze large cubes of ice and mounted a battery of 6- and 12-pounder cannon and a howitzer on them. Carleton's much heavier guns along the wall made short work of the American battery. Cannon balls and shells shattered the ice and dismounted Montgomery's guns.

Montgomery made one last try for a surrender. He sent Arnold and another officer toward the wall. They informed a messenger sent to meet them that they wished to speak to Carleton. They were told that the governor would neither see them nor accept a message.

Plans were then made for an attack. Montgomery was sending about 900 men against a garrison now increased to over 1,800, although many of the defenders were not first-class fighting men. Nevertheless, it was a desperate chance that had to be taken.

The plan of assault was a good one. Scaling ladders had been constructed. Carrying them, one American detachment was to advance on the Cape Diamond bastion and a second on the St. John's Gate, about midway between the main St. Louis Gate and the Palace Gate at the lower end of the wall. These attacks were simply to be feints to draw the British garrison to those points.

Meanwhile Arnold and his men, aided by forty of Captain John Lamb's artillery company, were to make their way into the Lower Town over the passage beyond the Palace Gate. At the same time Montgomery would lead the rest of the troops over the narrow strip of land at the foot of Cape Diamond. Both detachments were to meet in the Lower Town and force their way up the steep road to the Upper Town.

Surprise was of the greatest importance. If the two feints

at the wall deceived the British, Arnold's and Montgomery's detachments might be able to strike up the height from the Lower Town, attack Carleton's garrison from the rear and take Quebec.

What Montgomery needed was a dark, stormy night. The ill fortune that had dogged Arnold on his march continued on December 29 and 30, when all was in readiness. The weather was clear and, for a Quebec winter, mild. The next night was Montgomery's last chance.

Sunday, December 31, dawned fair, but by afternoon it was cloudy and the wind rose, bringing flurries of snow. By midnight there was a howling blizzard, with the snow two or three feet deep and piling up drifts.

At two in the morning, Arnold's men were summoned to Menut's Tavern. Technically, their enlistments had expired, but they obeyed the order. Captain Lamb's artillerymen also drew up with a 6-pounder cannon on a sled. Officers were hurrying in and out of the tavern. When the door swung open, a warm glow of light from within shone on the men outside on the black, snowswept plain. They stamped their feet against the cold while the snow drove like needles into their faces.

They waited until about four o'clock on the morning of that New Year's Day of 1776. The blizzard was at its height when signal rockets bright enough to be seen through the storm burst over the American lines. It was the summons to attack.

Arnold led his division of about 600 men down the slope. He was at the head of an advance group of twenty-five men—in military language, a "forlorn hope" whose chances of survival were poor. Next came Captain Lamb, his artillerymen and the 6-pounder. Morgan's sharpshooters followed and then the rest, including about forty French Canadians and Indians.

Carleton was not taken completely by surprise. An American deserter had warned him that Montgomery intended to strike in bad weather. The signal flares too had alerted the British. But at least the feints, although soon driven off, distracted the British attention to those points along the wall. Arnold's men passed the Palace Gate with no shots fired at them. More important, the barriers on the way from the Lower to the Upper Town were temporarily left unmanned.

Now the walls of the Rock rose sheer above Arnold's force. It was hard to push ahead through the blinding blizzard. The men covered the firelocks of their muskets with the folded edges of their coats to keep them clear of snow and dry. A storm of musket fire rattled down on them from the ramparts above, which were manned. And soon the artillerymen could no longer drag their one heavy gun on the sled through the drifts and had to abandon it.

The terrible punishment from the heights above lasted for almost a third of a mile. Some men were felled by bullets, although the number was miraculously small, probably because the enemy could not see their targets well. To add to the detachment's troubles, the cables of ships moored along the St. Lawrence shore were stretched across the way to houses huddled under the cliffs. Men tripped over them in the dark and fell flat, bruising themselves.

Suddenly the advance party shouted a warning and halted. Blocking the way was a barricade of heavy timbers. With a flash and a roar, one of the two heavy British cannon behind it fired. The gun was elevated too high, however, and the death-dealing grapeshot, filled with cast-iron balls, burst harmlessly in the rear. The second big gun fizzled when touched off and misfired.

Arnold shouted an order to rush the barrier. The men charged ahead, firing at the loopholes in the structure. Just then a musket ball ricocheted off a rock and hit Arnold in the leg below the knee. He staggered on for a few steps, shouting encouragement to the men, but he was bleeding heavily and leaving a red trail behind him in the snow.

Arnold was out of it. Already weak from loss of blood and supported by two men, he was taken back to the General Hospital. The command fell to Daniel Morgan, who shouted for a scaling ladder. One was placed against the barrier and the Virginian was up it in a trice, disappearing at the top in a cloud of musket smoke. Then the men saw him fall to the ground in front of the barrier.

They thought he was dead, but he was only stunned. In a moment he was on his feet, up the ladder again and over the barrier, yelling like an Indian warrior. He leaped down and rolled to safety under one of the British cannon until other Americans came tumbling over the barrier to take the position.

Ahead was a narrow, crooked street, the Sault au Matelot (Sailor's Leap), leading to the Lower Town. Perhaps two hundred yards beyond was another barrier. Its gate stood open, and the British behind it meekly surrendered.

The long, straggling American line followed Morgan through. There followed an incident much discussed by historians. Montgomery's orders had been that whichever of the two forces reached the Lower Town first should wait for the other. At that moment only a third, unmanned barrier lay ahead, and the Mountain Street barriers were also still undefended. If Morgan had plunged on immediately, he might have gained the Upper Town, caught the British garrison mainly in the rear and captured Quebec.

It was still dark as Morgan's force waited. And when Montgomery's troops did not appear, time ran out on the Virginian. Carleton had sent 200 men over the route Arnold had taken, to come up on the Americans from the rear. Others were plunging down Mountain Street to man the barriers there, as well as the last one in the Lower Town.

Most historians doubt that Morgan, if he had not stopped in the Lower Town, would have reached the Upper Town and taken it. But suppose Arnold had still been there? Morgan, great fighter that he was, tended always to obey orders. On occasion, as he proved later, Arnold was not one to consider orders if he saw a chance for glory ahead. He would probably have rampaged up the steep without waiting for Montgomery. Whether he would have captured Quebec is a question that can never be answered.

Where was Montgomery? The answer is a tragic one. He and his 300 men had made the precarious descent to Wolfe's Cove and along the equally difficult narrow strip of the shore, onto which the tides had pushed great masses of ice. Their progress was slowed by the cumbersome scaling ladders they carried.

At the foot of Cape Diamond they reached a barrier. It was deserted. Men with saws leaped to cut a passage through the big timbers. Montgomery, heading his own forlorn hope of fifty or sixty men, passed through. They went by a blockhouse, also deserted, and cut through another unmanned barrier. The way to the Lower Town seemed clear.

A house loomed ahead. In the darkness and snow it looked harmless, but it was loopholed and concealed fifty men—

British militia, loyal French Canadians, a ship captain and some sailors. Men with lighted matches stood by the cannon. As Montgomery came abreast of the house it erupted in a blast of grapeshot and musket balls. Richard Montgomery fell dead; a dozen others were raked down and lay in the blood-soaked snow. Colonel Donald Campbell, second in command, ordered a retreat, even though the Americans might have rushed and seized the house during the slow reloading of cannon and muskets.

That was the end. Too late, Daniel Morgan decided to assault the last barrier in the Lower Town. His men fought desperately and fiercely against odds. They were now beleaguered from front and rear. Finally, in order to save the lives of his men, Morgan surrendered.

Natanis's second legendary prediction had proved true. The Rock had defied the Dark Eagle.

SEVEN

Arnold Turns Admiral

The American attack on Quebec had been a disaster. The British killed or wounded about 60 men and captured 425, including 30 officers, as well as the abandoned 6-pounder cannon. These troops were almost entirely from Arnold's force. A few of his men did manage to escape over the treacherous ice of the St. Lawrence. Carleton had only eighteen casualties, five killed and thirteen wounded. Arnold, who as senior officer was now in command of the Americans, though he was still in the hospital, had about 600 men left, since a substantial number of French Canadians and Indians had joined his force. Soon afterward, however, more than a hundred Americans went home when their enlistments expired.

Arnold had no thought of giving up. When he had recovered sufficiently from his wound, he drew his troops back about a mile from the city, erected defenses of frozen snow and sent an urgent plea for reinforcements to Major General David Wooster, in command at Montreal. He was determined to have another try at Quebec.

Wooster, nearly sixty-four years old and cautious, at first refused to send any of the five or six hundred troops he had in Montreal. He was afraid the city's inhabitants would rise against him. Arnold's messenger went on to Albany. Although poor health had forced him to send General Montgomery in his place on the Quebec expedition, General Schuyler had remained in Albany in command of the Northern Continental Army. Schuyler could not help either. He had his hands full controlling Tory uprisings in the Mohawk River region, but he sent the messenger to Philadelphia with a letter to the Continental Congress asking that aid be sent to Arnold.

The Congress quickly voted to raise reinforcements in the northern colonies, asked Washington to send a battalion from Cambridge, appropriated $28,000 in hard money for Arnold to use, appointed him a brigadier general and sent him a letter praising his march to Quebec and his behavior in the assault. Meanwhile Wooster belatedly sent 120 men to Quebec, bringing Arnold's strength to between 600 and 700 men, although about 400 were in the hospital with smallpox.

Carleton, probably the ablest though least-known high-ranking British general in the Revolution, may have made a mistake in not taking advantage of the Americans' weakness. If he had sent his garrison out of Quebec, it might easily have annihilated Arnold's force or driven it into retreat. However, the British commander may have remembered what had happened to Montcalm in 1759 when he sallied out to meet Wolfe's British army.

Wooster finally summoned up the courage to send enough troops from Montreal to bolster the Americans' strength to about 2,000 men. But Wooster also came himself and took over the command, which must have been a bitter disappointment to Arnold. Arnold's chance for glory in a second assault on Quebec was now dimmed, and he did not get along with Wooster. When the wound in his leg was aggravated by bruises he suffered in a fall from his horse, he asked the new commander to transfer him to Montreal, and Wooster agreed. At least there, because of his rank, Arnold would have command of the city.

Arnold's disappointment is clearly shown in a letter he wrote Schuyler from Montreal. In it he said, "Had I been able to take an active part, I should have by no means left the camp; but as General Wooster did not think proper to consult me in any of his matters, I was convinced I should be of more service here than in camp."

Since Arnold had no part in the ill fortune that befell the American invading army for some months thereafter, these events may be summarized briefly. Wooster and his successor, Major General John Thomas, could do little more than try to harass the British until, early in May, fifteen British warships landed Major General John Burgoyne, one English and seven Irish regiments and 2,000 German mercenaries hired to fight for Britain. Carleton now had 13,000 men under his command.

He immediately sent out 900 troops to destroy the Americans. General Thomas's troops fled in a wild, disorderly retreat, abandoning all the artillery and stores of clothing, provisions, gunpowder and hospital equipment they had. The mud-covered, hungry, exhausted Americans did not stop until they reached Sorel. There they found temporary safety with a contingent of American troops supposed to go on to Quebec.

One bit of renown fell to Arnold before he left Montreal. Both General Thomas's troops and the reinforcements at Sorel were forced by the oncoming British to retreat up the Richelieu. Arnold left Montreal temporarily in the hands of Colonel

Moses Hazen, his second in command, and joined the retreating Americans to do what he could to help them reach safety.

Hazen meanwhile sent 400 men about thirty miles up the St. Lawrence to hold a small fortified post called the Cedars. Under a British Captain Forster, 150 English and Canadian troops and 500 Indians advanced on the Cedars. Major Isaac Butterfield, in charge at the defense post, made no attempt to defend it. He signed a surrender agreement under which the British agreed to protect the American prisoners from being butchered and scalped by Forster's Indians.

Arnold learned of Butterfield's surrender, assembled a large force and marched at once for the Cedars. In a towering rage he held a parley with Forster, demanding that the British yield the Cedars and the American prisoners. Forster countered with a threat to turn the Indians loose on the prisoners. Arnold told him that if he did so the Cedars would be overwhelmed and every British prisoner killed. Forster then backed down partially, refusing to give up the Cedars, although agreeing to a fair exchange of prisoners with those at Montreal. By this compromise Arnold saved 400 Americans.

In spite of the catastrophe at Quebec, the Americans were still determined to invade and conquer Canada. In June of 1776, 3,300 troops from New York and 2,000 from General Washington's army at Cambridge were sent into Canada to march against Quebec under command of Brigadier General John Sullivan.

Sullivan led 2,000 of his best troops against the first objective, the town of Trois Rivières, about halfway between Montreal and Quebec. Sullivan's information was that Trois Rivières was weakly defended by about 800 British regulars and Canadians. Actually, about 6,000 of an advance force of

8,000 men of Carleton's invasion army under Burgoyne had reached the town.

Sullivan's attack turned into a massacre of his men. They were routed, fled helter-skelter and were trapped in the swamps around Trois Rivières. About 400 Americans were killed and captured; only about a dozen British were killed or wounded.

Pursued by the whole British army under Carleton's command, the Americans at Sorel retreated up the Richelieu. Montreal was doomed and Arnold knew it. He could be reckless under the right circumstances, but to resist the advancing British would be to throw away his garrison's lives. He stayed as long as he dared and then evacuated the city. He himself was the last American to leave Montreal.

With the British on their heels, Sullivan's army moved up the Richelieu, past St. Johns, and halted at Ile aux Noix, a low-lying, swampy island in the river. Two thousand men were ill of smallpox and 1,500 or more suffering from dysentery or malaria; many died while the army rested in this unhealthy place for about two weeks. Meanwhile Arnold and his Montreal garrison had eluded the British and joined Sullivan. The Americans finally struggled back across the border to Crown Point, the starting point of Sullivan's ill-fated Canadian invasion.

The British halted their pursuit at St. Johns to prepare for their invasion of the colonies by way of Lake Champlain. Carleton planned to sail up Lake Champlain, invade the colonies and isolate New England, then join the army of Major General William Howe and the powerful British fleet at New York City. But he faced some difficult problems. He needed a fleet of his own to capture Crown Point and Ticonderoga and clear the way for his advance. What he learned of American preparations convinced him his armada must be powerful.

In the St. Lawrence the British had the three-masted ship *Inflexible*, mounting eighteen heavy 12-pounder cannon; the schooners *Maria* and *Carleton*, armed respectively with fourteen and twelve 6-pounders; and the *Loyal Convert*, a gondola propelled by both oars and sails, with seven 9-pounders. Also a British frigate had brought ten gunboats to Quebec that had been taken apart in England so that they could be shipped, each with bow guns ranging from 9-pounders to enormous 24-pounders.

Carleton had to get this fleet, along with a large number of smaller craft, to St. Johns. Just above the fort at Chambly and north of St. Johns were ten miles of rapids in the Richelieu. Impossible as it seemed to get the large warships past them, Carleton did it.

The three largest vessels were sailed up to Chambly. There they were placed on rollers so they could be dragged around the rapids, but the ground along the river was so swampy that the rollers sank into the mud under the weight of the warships. So Carleton had the vessels dismantled and the parts carried to St. Johns, where they were put back together. The rest of the armada was either dragged through the rapids or carried overland around them.

All this took time. Carleton recruited workmen and obtained tools and materials to reassemble the ships with all possible speed. A huge, flat-bottomed, raftlike affair named the *Thunderer* was also built at St. Johns. She mounted six 24-pounders, six 12-pounders and two howitzers. Three hundred men manned this formidable floating fortress.

Was there a chance that the tottering American army, part

of it at Crown Point, part at Ticonderoga, could do anything to stop Carleton? Except for Benedict Arnold, the answer would undoubtedly have been no.

Arnold's genius as a sea captain and his store of knowledge about ships and how they were built paid a rich reward to the American cause. Probably no other man in the Northern Continental Army could have accomplished what he did. Major General Horatio Gates, in command at Ticonderoga and Crown Point under Schuyler at Albany, knew of Arnold's naval qualifications and appointed him to assemble a fleet and to command it. In all respects, although he did not have the title, Arnold was now admiral of the Champlain fleet.

He did have the basis of a fleet already. In 1775 Montgomery had captured the British schooner *Royal Savage* on his march down the Richelieu. She mounted four 6-pounders and eight 4-pounders. When Allen took Ticonderoga, he had captured the British sloop *Enterprise*, with twelve 4-pounders. Taken at Skenesboro at that time was the schooner *Liberty*. Also the schooner *Revenge* had been built at Ticonderoga. Each schooner mounted four 4-pounders and two 2-pounders.

Arnold wanted more—gunboats and gondolas, each armed with one 12-pounder and two 9-pounders; sail- and oar-powered row galleys, each one with ten or twelve 18-, 12- and 9-pounders and manned by eighty men apiece, and other small craft. Building them was a prodigious task. There was plenty of timber, but hand tools for felling, hewing and sawing were limited to a few felling axes. There were few ship carpenters, sailmakers and riggers in the army. Three sawmills stood at Ticonderoga, Crown Point and Skenesboro, but they had been neglected and needed repair.

Arnold's boundless energy and leadership overcame every

difficulty. He had the sawmills repaired. He got 1,500 felling axes from Schuyler in Albany and 1,000 from Governor Jonathan Trumbull of Connecticut. He combed the army and dredged up a few ship and house carpenters. Schuyler helped out with a few more. This was not enough. Arnold sent urgent appeals to the New England seaports and even as far as Philadelphia. Two hundred ship carpenters with their tools came, as well as blacksmiths, sailmakers, riggers and oarmakers. They demanded outrageous wages in hard money. Somehow Arnold got the cash. The artisans built row-galleys and gondolas in a shipyard set up at Skenesboro.

All this sounds impressive, but it was little enough to oppose the mighty British fleet. Arnold was a David against a Goliath, but the American fleet was ready when Carleton's armada sailed from St. Johns on October 5. Some units of the American fleet sailed north as early as August 20. Arnold took the galley *Congress* as his flagship.

Twice Arnold arranged his ships in battle formation and twice he changed his mind. First, at Windmill Point, only two or three miles from the Canadian border, he strung the vessels in a line across the lake. Each was moored with an anchor that had a cable attached to its chain leading to the stern so that the vessel could be swung into any desired position. Then he sent men ashore to cut spruce trees and make fascines—bundles of small logs placed along the sides of the ships to help repel enemy boarding attempts and protect the men from small shot. The axmen were attacked; three were killed and six wounded by a scouting party of Carleton's Indians before a few cannon shots from the ships put the scouts to flight.

The fleet was anchored in a narrow part of the lake and

Arnold saw that the British might easily set up batteries on both sides to rake his ships with a devastating fire. He then moved to a wider anchorage alongside the Ile la Motte. This position still did not satisfy him and he moved farther south, looking for a place that would give him the advantage of concealment. About five miles below where curving Cumberland Head juts out from the New York shore was small Valcour Island. It rose high out of the water and was thickly forested. A narrow channel between the island and the shore looked like an ideal hiding place. Arnold sent men out in boats to take soundings of the channel. It was deep enough and the fleet moved in to wait.

The men of the fleet were all landsmen. With the sailor's scorn of landlubbers, Arnold wrote General Gates at Ticonderoga, demanding 200 sailors. "We have a wretched, motley crew in the fleet," he wrote, "the marines the refuse of every regiment and the seamen few of them ever wet with salt water." He also asked for some more experienced gunners, as well as warmer clothing, for cold weather was due soon in that northern region. He got none of the personnel or equipment he needed so badly.

Just in time, three galleys and two gondolas that had not been finished when Arnold sailed arrived at the anchorage. Now the American fleet was ready in its watery ambush, moored close together in a curving line, with the flagship *Congress* in the center. Arnold had 800 men to oppose Carleton's water-borne juggernaut, and thirty-two guns able to hurl a combined weight of 265 pounds of metal against the British fleet's fifty-three cannon firing a combined weight of about 500 pounds.

When Carleton sailed, he proceeded cautiously, knowing

the American fleet was ahead but not exactly where. His scouts had not discovered the Valcour Island hideaway. For his part, Arnold sent the *Revenge* out to reconnoiter; she returned to report that the British fleet was rounding Cumberland Head.

Brigadier General David Waterbury, who had directed the construction work under Arnold's supervision, was in command of the galley *Washington*. He urged Arnold to sail out and fight a retreating battle on the open lake against the British superiority. Arnold stuck to his plan to wait until Carleton's fleet reached the proper point and then give battle.

The moment the British ships came into view, Arnold ordered the *Royal Savage* and four galleys to attack. He followed in the *Congress*. He knew Carleton had a powerful fleet, but once he saw its might he realized the order had been a mistake and took the ships back to the cover of the channel. The British, making slow progress against a head wind, opened fire at long range, and the Americans returned it with all the guns they could bring to bear on their targets.

In trying to get back to the channel, the *Royal Savage* took three direct hits that slashed her sails and damaged a mast. Temporarily out of control, she ran aground on Valcour Island, but her gun crews kept on firing.

The big British warship *Inflexible* and the schooner *Maria* managed to beat within close range. They anchored and their guns, especially the *Inflexible*'s 12-pounders, blasted the American fleet with crippling broadsides. Then the *Carleton* and seventeen gunboats bore into the channel. They anchored in a line about 350 yards from Arnold's fleet, and a tremendous cannonade began. Until then everything had been preliminary maneuvering; now the real battle was on.

The British scored the first major blow. Their fire on the grounded *Royal Savage* forced her brave crew to abandon her. A boat's crew from the *Thunderer*—that floating arsenal was some distance off Valcour Island and never got into real action—boarded the *Royal Savage* and turned her guns against Arnold's fleet. American cannon fire drove the enemy party off, but finally a second British boat's crew from the *Maria* set her afire. Her powder magazine blew up and destroyed her.

It was the Americans' turn for one of their few triumphs in the battle. Their guns' fury was turned on the *Carleton*. Arnold himself, who knew more about gunnery than anyone else in the fleet, sighted the *Congress*'s guns. The *Carleton* was hit so many times that all her senior officers were put out of action and a young midshipman took command. The American broadsides continued for hours until a ball shot away a spring cable on the *Carleton*, causing her to swing so that the American fire could rake her from stem to stern. At last two British boats got alongside and managed to tow her away, with half her crew killed or wounded and two feet of water in the hold.

The late afternoon of October 11 was waning when the *Inflexible* maneuvered into very close range of Arnold's fleet. She fired five deadly broadsides into the American line of ships and silenced all its guns. But instead of following up this advantage, the *Inflexible* and the line of British gunboats withdrew.

The Americans' plight was nevertheless desperate. Twelve balls had penetrated the hull of the *Congress*, and her mainmast had been hit twice. The *Washington* galley had taken a terrible shelling. An hour after that first day's battle, the

Philadelphia gondola sank, hulled by many shots. The entire fleet's sails were in tatters, sixty Americans had been killed or wounded, and three-quarters of the ammunition was gone.

It seemed a hopeless situation. All Carleton's fleet had to do in the morning was to sail in and either demolish what was left of the American flotilla or receive its surrender. Most commanders would have yielded in order to save their men's lives. Not Arnold. Never once while in a Revolutionary battle did he give up. He simply did not recognize the word "defeat." That night he proved his dauntlessness.

Under cover of darkness and a thick fog, Arnold's fleet limped out of the channel in a single line. On the stern of each ship was fixed a hooded lantern, invisible to the British but able to guide the vessel astern of her. Once these craft were clear of Carleton's fleet, the oars were shipped aboard the vessels that had them and the oarsmen pulled on them all through the night up the lake.

By dawn the line was long and straggling, with the *Enterprise, Revenge, Liberty*, the galley *Lee* and five gondolas ahead. Astern of them, two other galleys, the *Congress* and *Washington*, and the gondolas *Providence, New York* and *New Jersey* put in at small Schuyler's Island in a desperate effort to make repairs. The *New York* and *Providence* were in such bad shape that they were sunk after all usable equipment was taken off. The *New Jersey* had run aground and was abandoned. The two galleys, with Arnold aboard the *Congress*, then continued the race for safety in the afternoon.

That morning of October 12 Carleton was so surprised, infuriated and confused to find that the fox had eluded his dogs of war that for a time his wits deserted him. He started a swift chase but forgot to send orders to the British troops making their way overland up the lake to proceed and had to turn back, losing precious time.

Even so, the race was close. The American galleys had to depend on their oars against a southerly head wind, while the British fleet had the benefit of a northerly wind coming up the lake. The British soon came within range of the American ships and riddled them with grape and round shot. Two galleys were quickly in trouble. General Waterbury, commanding the *Washington*, had to strike his flag and surrender. The galley *Lee*, which had been among the craft in the lead, was captured when she ran aground and was abandoned.

The *Congress* and four of the five gondolas, which had been among the leaders in the fleeing line but had fallen back, were still safe, since the north wind caught up with them. They continued the unequal, utterly hopeless fight for two and a half hours. Three British warships directed their fire on Arnold's *Congress*. She was staggering now, barely afloat, her sails cut to ribbons. But Arnold did not surrender. He signaled the crews on the gondolas to turn with him for the east shore of the lake, where they beached the five battered wrecks, set them afire, waited till they were sure the powder magazines would blow up and then started overland on a ten-mile march toward Crown Point. They discovered an Indian ambush ahead of them and eluded it. When they reached Crown Point, darkness had fallen. There what was left of the *Enterprise*, *Liberty*, *Revenge*, the galley *Trumbull* and one gondola that had outdistanced the enemy had arrived safely.

There was no use in trying to hold Crown Point. The Americans burned its buildings and retreated to stronger Ticonderoga.

Sir Guy Carleton was a gallant as well as an able general.

At Ticonderoga British rowboats approached under a flag of truce. They carried General Waterbury and the 110 men of the surrendered *Washington*. It was as if Carleton had made the generous gesture in tribute to Arnold's naval genius.

Twelve ships of the American fleet had been lost, along with eighty men. Although Arnold had suffered a crushing defeat, he nevertheless had won a victory. He had saved the American colonists from almost certain defeat.

The long delay while the British fleet was being assembled at St. Johns and the fight at Valcour Island had sealed the fate of Carleton's invasion. Approaching Ticonderoga, he faced a crucial decision. He must capture the fortress before he could go on to Albany. How long would it take? In all probability it could not be taken by quick assault. A siege might last through the winter's storms and bitter cold, and Carleton's nearest base of supplies was at Quebec, three hundred miles away. Even if he did take the fortress fairly soon, he could not push on to the Hudson and Albany in the winter. His army could easily find itself trapped.

Carleton decided against taking the chance and withdrew to Quebec. Benedict Arnold had given the Americans a year of delay before the British could invade again.

One of the greatest authorities on naval science, Admiral Alfred Thayer Mahan, later wrote: "That the Americans were strong enough to impose the capitulation of Saratoga was due to the invaluable year of delay secured to them in 1776 by their little navy on Lake Champlain, created by the indomitable energy, and handled with the indomitable courage of the traitor, Benedict Arnold."

The Dark Eagle had begun his soaring flight toward the sky.

EIGHT

Humiliation
and More Glory

Since there could be no military action in the Lake Champlain area during the winter, Arnold wanted to go to New Haven and see his sister and the children. He rode to Albany, where he was delayed when two enemies seeking his disgrace brought charges against him. Major John Brown charged Arnold with thirteen military "crimes," but nothing came of the accusations. Arnold had often clashed with his second in command at Montreal, Lieutenant Colonel Moses Hazen, and had had him court-martialed for insubordination. Hazen had been found not guilty, and now he declared that Arnold had insulted his character; this was brought before a court of inquiry, which found that Hazen's complaint was "just," although Arnold suffered no punishment. Nevertheless, both cases wounded his pride severely and he did not forget them.

Early in December 1776 he left for New Haven. His fame was by then so great in Connecticut that the journey through his native state was a triumphal procession, which eased his hurt feelings somewhat. He remained with his family for a short time, but before Christmas he was off to Providence, Rhode Island, on orders from General Washington.

In New York, General Howe, having driven Washington's army into retreat southward through New Jersey, was so confident of finishing off the rebels quickly that he sent Major General Henry Clinton with more than 6,000 troops to take over Newport, Rhode Island, for a naval base. Clinton easily occupied Newport. Arnold thought he could drive the British out of Newport and went from Providence to Boston, where he tried to raise troops for the attack. Washington finally told Arnold that unless he could put a strong enough force in the field to make the expedition's success absolutely certain he must remain on the defensive. Arnold reluctantly gave up his plan.

While he was in Boston, Arnold fell in love with Betsy Deblois. Although she was the daughter of a Loyalist who had fled to Nova Scotia when the British evacuated the town in March 1776, Betsy had remained in Boston. Arnold wrote her a passionate letter imploring her to favor him as her suitor. She did not return his affection, however, and the affair ended.

In February 1777 Arnold suffered another blow to his pride. It was one of a number of slights during his military career that helped to sow the seeds of treason in his mind. On February 19, 1777, the Continental Congress appointed five new major generals. All five had been brigadier generals like Arnold, but all were junior to him and all vastly inferior in military ability.

Congress had not bothered to consult Washington in making the appointments, and the commander in chief was deeply disturbed. He wrote one of the members in Philadelphia expressing his shock and disappointment that Arnold had been overlooked and added, "... it is not to be presumed (being the oldest brigadier) that he will continue in service under such a slight."

Arnold felt that the five brigadiers had been promoted over his head because they had more political influence in the Continental Congress. He decided to go and face his enemies in Philadelphia. But first he made a short stopover in New Haven to see Hannah and the boys again.

In that April of 1777 in New York City, General Howe commissioned William Tryon, royal governor of the partly British-held colony, to take a force of 2,000 men, mostly British regulars, to Danbury, Connecticut, and destroy a large American depot of stores there. Tryon did the job thoroughly and then headed back toward Long Island Sound, where his transports were waiting to take the expedition back to New York.

American forces swarmed in to meet Tryon. General Wooster and Brigadier General Gold Silliman marched with 100 Continental troops and 500 Connecticut militia. Arnold promptly forgot his sulks, mounted a horse and galloped to join them.

The best Wooster and Silliman hoped to do was to harass Tryon during his withdrawal toward the Sound. Arnold had other ideas. With 200 men he raced ahead of the British and blocked the two roads by which Tryon could escape.

A British flanking force got around to the rear of Arnold's barriers, forcing him to order a retreat. A British platoon that surged in fired a volley at Arnold from only about thirty yards away. His horse fell dead, carrying Arnold, entangled in his stirrups, to the ground. A soldier charged down on him with bayonet fixed, crying, "Surrender! You are my prisoner."

"Not yet!" Arnold shouted. In spite of his predicament he drew a pistol and shot the man dead.

The main British force got around the barriers but were forced to make a defensive stand on a hill. Inspired by Arnold's shouts of encouragement, the whole American force advanced to attack, but a furious British bayonet charge broke their ranks and Tryon was able to reach his transports. At least, due to Arnold's leadership and bold tactics, the British lost about 150 in killed and wounded and the Americans only 60, including old General Wooster, who was killed.

Word of Arnold's heroism spread rapidly and reached Philadelphia. On May 2 Congress appointed him a major general, although it did not make him senior to the other five major generals.

Arnold resumed his journey to Philadelphia. He was determined to clear himself fully of Brown's charges of thirteen military "crimes," which included seizing captured goods at Montreal for Arnold's own use. Several members of the Continental Congress came to his aid. One of his supporters, John Adams, in a letter to his wife wrote, "I spent last evening at the war office with General Arnold. He has been basely slandered and libeled."

The delegates became convinced that Brown's charges were false. Arnold was cleared of them, and Congress voted to present him with a finely caparisoned horse "as a token of their appreciation of his gallant conduct in the action against the enemy in their late enterprize to Danbury." But the delegates still did nothing to make Arnold senior to the other five new major generals. This neglect, combined with his outrage over the investigation of his accounts during the Quebec expedition and the retreat to Lake Champlain (even though nothing was found wrong with them), left Arnold further dissatisfied with his treatment at the hands of Congress.

Now Washington had need of Arnold's talents with the Northern Continental Army. A new British invasion from Canada was under way.

Carleton's retreat after the battle of Valcour Island had brought him into the bad graces of British Secretary of State for the Colonies, Lord George Germain. Germain, who most incompetently handled the British side of the Revolution from London, did not understand or appreciate what Carleton had faced before Ticonderoga. And because of Germain's prejudice against him, the able Carleton never again led a British army in the field in America.

"Gentleman Johnny" Burgoyne, the handsome, dashing and most colorful of all British generals in America during the Revolution, also was in ill favor with Germain because he had supported Carleton's decision to withdraw from Lake Champlain. This did not bother Burgoyne in the least, for King George III of Britain was his good friend. When he returned to England, he went directly to the king with a proposal for another British invasion of the colonies from Canada over the same route on which Carleton had started in 1776. George III liked the plan and appointed Burgoyne to command the expedition.

Burgoyne arrived at Quebec on May 6, 1777. In June he was at St. Johns. His expedition started with about 7,600 men: approximately 3,700 British infantrymen, 3,000 Brunswick and Hessian mercenaries, 400 artillerymen, 150 French Canadians and 400 Indians. They were not quite as well equipped as Burgoyne had expected, especially since he lacked enough horses to mount the German dragoons. Altogether, however, it was a powerful force, with an excellent fleet at St. Johns.

The expedition proceeded according to Burgoyne's plan with little trouble at first, and easily captured Fort Ticonderoga. Then Burgoyne detached a force of 875 men to capture American-held Fort Stanwix in the valley of the Mohawk River. He felt this must be done to put down any trouble with the Americans in the region who might hamper his southward invasion.

Under command of Lieutenant Colonel Barry St. Leger, who was given the temporary rank of brigadier general, this British force went up the St. Lawrence and Lake Ontario to Oswego in far western New York. There it was joined by between 800 and 1,000 Six Nations Indians led by the famous Mohawk chief Joseph Brant.

The expedition reached Stanwix on August 2, 1777. In the fort were 750 determined defenders commanded by Colonel Peter Gansevoort. St. Leger sent in a demand for surrender. Gansevoort did not even bother to answer it. St. Leger then laid siege to the fort.

Word that the expedition was on its way to the Mohawk Valley had made the many Tories in the region bolder in their resistance to the American patriots. As early as July 17 Brigadier General Nicholas Herkimer of the Tryon County militia had issued an appeal to all able-bodied patriots in the valley to be ready to defend their homes. They responded enthusiastically. On July 30 Herkimer learned that St. Leger was approaching Fort Stanwix. On August 4 he marched at the head of about 800 volunteers from Fort Dayton on the Mohawk River, about thirty miles below Stanwix.

Herkimer planned to relieve the besieged garrison at the fort. He sent four scouts ahead to tell Gansevoort he was coming. In turn, when Gansevoort was ready, he was to fire three cannon shots as a signal that he was about to send a detachment out to engage St. Leger's force. Herkimer's men would then rush in so that the British would be attacked from front and rear.

It was the best kind of military tactics, and Herkimer, the son of German immigrants, was Arnold's kind of fighting man, completely fearless, but without Arnold's reckless streak. As his column advanced and no shots were heard, he concluded Gansevoort was not ready and decided to halt and wait. His officers, however, demanded that Herkimer go ahead anyway and called him a coward for his caution. He finally yielded to them against his better judgment.

He had some Oneida Indians with him. The Oneidas were one of the two Six Nations tribes who had not joined with the British. Herkimer sent sixty of them ahead to reconnoiter. Ordinarily such scouts would have discovered the ambush that St. Leger had set up in Herkimer's path but they missed it. Perhaps if Herkimer had waited, the Indians would have discovered the trap.

Along the route lay a ravine fifty feet deep with a small stream running at its bottom, bordered by swamp. Through the ravine ran a corduroy road made of logs that Herkimer's force had to pass over. A few British soldiers, some Tory rangers and 400 of Joseph Brant's Indians were concealed nearby.

As Herkimer's column was coming through the ravine, the Indians leaped from their cover and fell upon them. Herkimer, in the lead and near the opposite rim of the ravine, turned and galloped back as the British in the ambush joined the battle. Herkimer's horse was shot dead, and he was seriously wounded in the leg.

The enemy completely surrounded the Americans and everything pointed to a massacre. In spite of his wound, which made him unable to walk, Herkimer sat down under a tree and calmly directed his men's defense as he smoked his pipe. He ordered them to form in a compact circle and fight for their lives. They did, using clubbed muskets in a desperate stand against British gunfire and the tomahawks and scalping knives of the Indians.

The Americans were saved when a torrential rainstorm began, soaking the musket priming of both sides so that no gun could be fired during the downpour. It gave Herkimer a chance to have his men take cover behind trees in pairs so that one man could fire while the other was reloading when fighting resumed.

The storm ended as suddenly as it had begun, and the Americans then did better. Their fire caused many casualties among the Indians. Even though some Tory reinforcements came up to join the fight, the surviving Indians fled into the forest around the ravine and vanished. The Tory troops followed. The Americans had won what came to be known as the battle of Oriskany, but they could not give chase to the enemy since they had to take care of fifty or so wounded men, including the dauntless Herkimer, who later died of his wound.

Meanwhile the siege of Fort Stanwix went on. Herkimer's messengers had arrived too late for Gansevoort to fire his signal guns and send out his force against St. Leger. The British cannon were too light to batter down the fort's walls at long range, so St. Leger began to close in by digging parallel trenches, each one nearer the fort's walls.

Word of St. Leger's siege reached Schuyler at his headquarters in Stillwater, on the Hudson River south of Saratoga. He decided that Fort Stanwix must be relieved and called a council of war. Most of his officers objected to the idea because they felt that the Northern Continental Army was already too weak to meet the oncoming Burgoyne.

Schuyler was so angry that he bit the stem of his clay pipe in two. He said, "Gentlemen, I shall take the responsibility upon myself. Fort Stanwix and the Mohawk Valley shall be saved! Where is the brigadier who will command the relief?"

Arnold, who had strongly supported Schuyler's plan, instantly volunteered. Other volunteers among the soldiers gave him a force of 350 men, who were joined on the march by 100 of the Tryon County militia. Arnold could be cautious when circumstances required it, and having heard that St. Leger had 1,700 men besieging Stanwix, he proceeded slowly. When word reached him that the fort was in grave danger, however, his boldness overcame the caution. He began a forced march with all possible speed.

Arnold was not destined to fight St. Leger, although he would have been glad to. He had devised a clever scheme to deceive his enemy. Hon Yost, a German civilian who supported the British, had been arrested for trying to recruit men for them and was sentenced to death. Arnold promised to pardon Yost if he would go to St. Leger's camp and report that an overwhelming American force was approaching.

Arnold's men cunningly prepared Hon Yost for his mission. They took his coat and put several bullets through it. Then, accompanied by an Oneida, who probably was to make sure there would be no treachery, the German set out. He went alone into the camp of St. Leger's Indians outside Fort Stanwix and told them he had barely escaped Arnold's expedition, showing the bullet holes in his coat. He said thousands of American troops were about to attack. The Indians took him to St. Leger, to whom he reported that he had escaped the Americans while on his way to the gallows.

Yost's Oneida companion then went among the Indians and repeated the story of the approaching big American army. The Indians began preparations to leave. Even St. Leger's other troops became panic-stricken. The Indians then rioted, seizing officers' supplies of liquor and clothing. Two hundred of them fled and the remaining chiefs demanded a retreat.

St. Leger yielded. His force was so frightened that it left behind its tents, artillery, ammunition and supplies and made a headlong flight toward Oswego.

Arnold had relieved Fort Stanwix without losing a single man. At Stillwater Schuyler was overjoyed to have the troops back. As for Burgoyne, he would sorely miss St. Leger's force, which he had expected to join him before he met the Northern Continental Army.

NINE

Saratoga

Burgoyne's good judgment in ordering St. Leger's mission is doubtful. Tory resistance to American patriots in the Mohawk Valley was well organized. The Loyalists from that region were prepared to meet the local patriots' resistance to Gentleman Johnny's main force on its invasion route.

But Burgoyne made a more serious mistake when, after easily taking Fort Ticonderoga, he sent 800 Germans, British regulars, Tories, Canadians and Indians to Bennington on the New Hampshire Grants to seize horses to mount his dragoons and to obtain cattle and other food supplies.

Burgoyne had been told that the farmers at Bennington would run at the sight of an enemy uniform. Instead, the farmers, with the assistance of New Hampshire militia under capable Major General John Stark, gave the invaders a terrible beating. Although 600 reinforcements had been sent hurrying to support the British expedition, over 200 of Burgoyne's army were killed and about 700 captured with all their equipment. Only about 30 Americans were killed and 40 wounded. Burgoyne needed those lost troops as badly as those of St. Leger's expedition.

A third and most serious mistake was the pompous manifesto Burgoyne issued to the inhabitants along his invasion route. He warned them that unless they gave no aid to the American rebels and cooperated fully with his own army he had "but to give stretch to the Indian forces under my direction," adding untruthfully, "(and they amount to thousands)." This threat of massacre so infuriated the people of the region that hundreds flocked to join Schuyler's American army.

A worse result of the manifesto was yet to come. Jane McCrea, a young woman of twenty-three living near Saratoga, went north to Fort Edward as Burgoyne's troops approached that abandoned American defense post. There she expected to meet her fiance, a Tory who had joined Burgoyne. A group of Indians swooped down on Fort Edward, seized Jane McCrea and a Mrs. McNeill, with whom Jane was staying, and carried them off toward Burgoyne's camp at Fort Ann. On the way a dispute arose between two Indians over possession of the captives. One of them shot Jane McCrea dead and scalped her.

Although Jane McCrea was obviously a Loyalist, this made no difference to the outraged inhabitants. It seemed that Burgoyne had "given stretch" to his Indians, and he was going to pay dearly for it. More hundreds of volunteers swarmed into the Northern Continental Army's camp.

Meanwhile the Americans had a setback. General Gates wanted command of the Northern Continental army. Since he had more political influence with the Continental Congress in Philadelphia than Schuyler, he was able to elbow Schuyler out of the command. Gates was an incompetent general, however, and later showed himself a coward after his army was routed by the British at Camden, South Carolina.

When Burgoyne approached Saratoga, Gates's army had about 7,000 men. Thanks to Burgoyne's ill-advised manifesto and the tragedy of Jane McCrea, the American strength was superior to the opposing army of something over 6,000. The difference was balanced, however, by Burgoyne's battle-seasoned British regulars and the German professional fighting men.

As Burgoyne's army moved to within a few miles of Saratoga, Gates selected his battleground. He chose the area of Bemis Heights, a little southeast of Saratoga itself. Bemis Heights stood on a bluff that rose steeply more than a hundred feet from the Hudson River. A plateau north of the bluff was still higher and cut by several ravines, with the Great Ravine the deepest and widest of them. Most of the ground was forested except for a few clearings.

It was a good choice. On Bemis Heights a three-sided defense work was erected, with the edge of the bluff as the fourth side of a square. A bridge of boats was thrown across the river so that the Americans could retreat over it if necessary.

From Fort Miller, on the east side of the river, Burgoyne crossed over. Since most of his Indian scouts had deserted him, he did not know exactly where the Americans were until he was within a few miles of them.

The "battle of Saratoga" was actually two battles. The first, known as Freeman's Farm, took place on September 19, 1777, about a mile north of Gates's headquarters in the redoubt on the bluff. Burgoyne stationed two of the three wings of his offensive line south of the Great Ravine, spread wide apart. The right wing, under Brigadier General Simon Fraser, was just west of the ravine. Burgoyne hoped this wing could reach an elevation just northwest of and near the American earthworks on the bluff and fire down on them.

Benedict Arnold commanded the American left wing, which faced Fraser's strong right, with its 2,000 British, Brunswickers, Canadians and Tory troops plus a few Indians. Arnold was eager to strike at the enemy, but Gates, remaining within the Bemis Heights defenses, gave no orders at all. When Arnold implored Gates to let him attack, the army's commander did send Colonel Morgan and some light infantry from Arnold's wing to prevent Fraser from getting around the American left flank.

Burgoyne planned to wait until Fraser had gained the elevation near Bemis Heights and then send the rest of his army forward. His left wing, 1,100 strong and commanded by Major General William Phillips, was composed of Brunswick infantry regiments and Hessian artillery. The center, accompanied by Burgoyne himself, was also made up of 1,100 men of British regiments with six light field artillery pieces. The rest of the army was in reserve in the rear.

At one o'clock that afternoon Burgoyne was apparently convinced that Fraser's troops had gained the high ground, and he ordered the other wings of his front line to advance. Gentleman Johnny was wrong in his belief. Morgan's riflemen had routed a strong detachment of Fraser's troops, although the Americans too had been scattered when a strong Tory force, also under Fraser, fell upon them. But the high ground remained unoccupied.

The battle was raging now all along the opposing lines. Its tide shifted constantly, the advantage now with the Americans, now with the British. Then, from his position on the field, Arnold detected a weakness in Burgoyne's center. If he could get reinforcements, he could cut this line in two. He galloped swiftly to headquarters and begged Gates for more men.

It is quite understandable that two generals as different as Gates and Arnold should not get along well, and they did not. Gates refused Arnold's demand, saying it would "weaken his lines." Arnold gave him such a hot argument that he did send out a brigade, but he ordered Arnold not to return to the battle. It was a foolish order.

Under Arnold's leadership the one brigade might have broken Burgoyne's center; without him it failed. Then, when German Major General Baron von Riedesel and his own regiment charged into the thick of the battle, the Americans began to falter. If darkness had not fallen, Burgoyne might have won the battle, even the Revolution itself. As it was, neither side was the victor, although 600 of Burgoyne's troops had been killed, captured or wounded, while Gates's army had lost only 65 killed, 218 wounded and 36 missing.

The next day could have proved a different story, for the Americans' ammunition was running short. But for no apparent reason Burgoyne did not resume hostilities on September 20. And on September 21 he received a dispatch from Sir Henry Clinton (who had been knighted for his success on Long Island) that caused a much longer delay.

Clinton was temporarily in command of the British troops in New York City. Before Burgoyne left England, Lord Germain had promised to send General Howe a dispatch directing him to cooperate from New York City with Burgoyne's expedition. Either Germain neglected or forgot for a time to send the message. By the time it reached Howe, the British commander in chief had left New York with a large force to engage General Washington's army in Pennsylvania and capture Philadelphia.

Clinton's dispatch to Burgoyne said he was coming up the Hudson to capture Fort Montgomery near Peekskill. Burgoyne naturally thought that this was the help from Howe that he had been expecting. He decided to wait for Clinton to arrive and then crush the Northern Continental Army.

The delay was a great boon to the Americans. More volunteers arrived at Gates's camp; his defenses were strengthened, and more ammunition obtained.

Meanwhile Clinton captured Fort Montgomery and sent Burgoyne another dispatch. To Gentleman Johnny's great chagrin, the message simply wished him luck but contained no promise of aid; in fact, Clinton sailed back to New York City.

During this interval of over two weeks Burgoyne's strength, what with his losses at Freeman's Farm and a great many desertions, was reduced to only about 5,000 men. On the other hand, Gates's army had swelled to about 11,000. Moreover, Burgoyne's supply of food was running low.

At a British council of war it was decided to resume the battle and send a force of 1,500 to probe the American left wing. Burgoyne and his officers felt that this was the weakest point of the enemy's line. If the probing force made headway, the rest of the army would launch an attack on the other American wings. Burgoyne's strategy was a gamble, but he had only the choice of resuming the battle or retreating with his invasion a failure.

In spite of the advantage the Americans had gained during the long lull, things were going badly in their camp. Gates and Arnold were like two hostile dogs, each watching his chance to sink his fangs in the other. The dispute caused disruption and ill feeling among the other officers, although almost all of Gates's staff favored Arnold.

The disagreement flared into open hostility when the two got into a bitter quarrel. The enraged Gates issued an order relieving Arnold from all command and directing him to leave the camp. If Gates's behavior toward Arnold during the battle of Freeman's Farm had been foolish, this vengeful blow at him was little short of idiotic.

The officers who supported Arnold were incensed. They drew up a letter urging him to remain, and without Gates's knowledge Arnold did. Meanwhile Major General Benjamin Lincoln was appointed in his place.

The second battle of Saratoga, known as Bemis Heights, began on the morning of October 7. Burgoyne sent out the reconnoitering party from his right wing. It was composed of Captain John Fraser's rangers and a group of 600 Canadians and Indians. It made a wide sweep to the right in an attempt to divert the Americans in that direction. Nothing of the sort happened.

When word of this strategic move reached American headquarters, Daniel Morgan, who had been on the American left under Arnold and still was there, suggested that his riflemen attack the now weakened British right wing. Gates agreed. He also ordered Brigadier General Enoch Poor to strike at the British left wing. Both forces were to advance, hidden from view, through forest and strike at the same time.

Poor's force of about 800 met British grenadiers under Major John Acland who were established on a slight elevation. As the Americans advanced up the slope, the British gave them a heavy fire of musketry, but most of it was aimed too high. The Americans held their fire until Acland ordered a bayonet charge. Poor's men then gave the enemy a deadly volley. Acland fell, shot through both legs. The Americans seized a 12-pounder British cannon and turned it against their foes. The British were thrown into retreat, and Acland was captured.

Meanwhile Morgan had gone into action against the light infantry on the British right wing, commanded by the Earl of Balcarres and stationed behind a rail fence. The Virginia riflemen advanced into a hail of musket and grapeshot fire and hurled themselves on the enemy; they were supported by light infantry that had come up to aid them. Balcarres's men turned and fled, abandoning their heavy guns. The rest of the British right wing followed them.

So far, Gates's plan was working perfectly. Burgoyne saw that his whole army was endangered. He sent out an order to withdraw, but the messenger was shot and captured on the way.

Left now with no support was the British center, composed of Brunswickers commanded by General Riedesel. The professional, battle-seasoned soldiers were ready to fight it out, and the Americans, led by Brigadier General Ebenezer Learned, advanced cautiously toward the Germans.

Suddenly a small man in a general's uniform galloped out of the Bemis Heights fortification. It was Benedict Arnold. He had seen Learned's caution and it was not to his liking. He himself had thrown caution away as far as Gates's dismissal of him was concerned. He took over the command, while the soldiers behind him raised a tremendous cheer. With Arnold leading them, they soon forgot any fears.

Gates, who had seen Arnold ride out of the redoubt, was

beside himself with anger. "He may do some rash thing," he said, and he sent an aide out to order his enemy off the field. But Arnold outdistanced the messenger and stayed in the fight.

The Brunswickers had been reinforced by Hessian regiments and stood their ground. Arnold's men could not withstand the torrent of fire poured in on them and they were repulsed. Undaunted, Arnold led a second charge on the Germans until, when about to be surrounded, the Brunswickers were ordered to retreat.

British General Fraser had been all over the field, encouraging the troops. Now he attempted to form a new British defense line. Arnold saw what he was doing. To Morgan, at his side, he said, "That man on the gray horse is a host in himself and must be disposed of."

Morgan sent one of his crack shots up a tree to pick Fraser off. From his precarious position in the branches the marksman fired twice and missed. One of Fraser's aides told him he was the target of the shots and should withdraw. Fraser replied that it was his duty to remain. A moment later the sharpshooter's third shot mortally wounded this brave Britisher.

The battle should have ended then, for the second British line collapsed and retreated to Burgoyne's breastworks in the rear. Arnold was not satisfied, however. Burgoyne might retreat and at least save his army. So Arnold led two brigades in an assault on a British redoubt at the western end of the Great Ravine and then brought Learned's brigade up. The Americans surrounded the redoubt, which was occupied by Brunswickers.

Arnold rode to the rear and entered the redoubt through its sally port. There his horse was shot dead, and he was seriously wounded in the same leg that had been injured at Quebec. At Saratoga the bullet broke his thigh bone.

When the German commander, Lieutenant Colonel Heinrich Breymann, was mortally wounded, the redoubt was surrendered. But for approaching darkness and Arnold's being out of action, the Americans might have overwhelmed the rest of Burgoyne's army. As it was, the British commander had lost about 600 men—killed, wounded or captured—and all his cannon. The American casualties were about 150.

Burgoyne withdrew his army to a position north of the Great Ravine near the bluffs over the Hudson and threw up new redoubts. Gates had 2,000 New Hampshire militia on an elevation north of Fort Edward, and he ordered 1,300 Massachusetts militia to cross the Hudson, go north, come back over and entrench themselves at Saratoga. Thus Burgoyne had enemy forces both in front and to his rear to block a retreat.

Burgoyne was informed of the American movements, and he countered by withdrawing still farther to the heights near Saratoga. He had had a fleet of bateaux to ferry his army across the Hudson and thus evade the enemy forces on the west side, but the Americans had captured most of the boats. The British commander called a council of war on October 12 at which five plans for possible further action were discussed. The officers could agree on none of them until General Riedesel insisted that the only workable solution was to abandon their baggage and retreat northward by night.

Still Burgoyne hesitated. He gave no orders to march that night and the delay meant his doom, for the next day his army was entirely surrounded by the Americans. Then, at another council of war, it was decided that if an honorable surrender could be arranged, it was the best thing to do.

Gates gave Burgoyne the most generous of terms, probably because he had heard rumors that Clinton was on his way up the Hudson. The defeated troops were not to be considered prisoners of war, but marched to Boston, where transportation to England would be arranged, while the Canadians were to be allowed to go home. The surrender was to be carried out with all the honors of war.

On October 17, 1777, both armies were drawn up at the American camp. Burgoyne advanced to a tent and handed his sword to Gates, who took it, bowed and returned it. The Northern Continental Army had won the greatest victory of the Revolution up to that time. It had put 5,000 enemy troops out of the war and captured enormous stores of guns of all sizes, ammunition, supplies and equipment. Even more important, the victory had injected new heart and confidence into the supporters of the American cause. The Americans would yet suffer serious reverses, but Saratoga turned the tide in their favor for the first time. The battle also had a strong effect in swinging France over as an active American ally. Altogether it was a victory of stupendous consequence.

Gates, of course, received official credit for it. He has been criticized for remaining in his Bemis Heights headquarters throughout the Freeman's Farm and Bemis Heights battles, but in the kind of engagement the Americans were fighting, it was his proper station. Some of his strategy was excellent, but his weakness lay in his indecision, his reluctance to risk the safety of the troops with him in the redoubt and especially his shortsighted dismissal of Arnold.

It was Arnold, by his disobedience to Gates and his reckless charge on the redoubt, who forced Burgoyne to withdraw farther and sealed the British general's fate. Some historians claim Arnold's spectacular entrance into the battle was of no importance because Saratoga was already won. Save for Arnold's action, however, Burgoyne would probably have tried another attack. The evidence is strong that Arnold was chiefly responsible for forcing Burgoyne's surrender, although credit is also due to the indomitable Morgan and other generals for carrying out their parts in the fighting so well.

Benedict Arnold's wings had indeed brushed the sky. As the legend has it, Natanis predicted that when this happened an arrow would pierce the Dark Eagle's heart. That arrow began its flight when Arnold and his men entered the enemy redoubt and Arnold fell, wounded again in his bad leg.

TEN

Treason

Benedict Arnold's wound healed slowly, and he was a bad patient during the weeks he spent in the hospital in Albany, fretting and ill-tempered. He was eager to get back into action, win more laurels and show the politicians in Congress who had treated him so badly that they owed him an apology and elevation to the higher rank he deserved.

By January 11, 1778, Arnold was able to sit up, but he had to stay in the hospital until he could hobble about on a crutch. During that time Congress did make amends. It voted to promote him to major general, with the date of his advancement, February 17, 1777, making him senior to the five other brigadiers promoted over his head. This mollified Arnold somewhat, although the wounds to his feelings over what his enemies in the Continental Army had done to him were as deep as the wound in his leg. He had not forgotten the actions of Brown, Hazen, Gates and others.

In the early spring Arnold was able to leave for Connecticut. For several weeks he rested at Middletown at the home of a merchant–shipowner he had known well in the old days. While he was there, Betsy Deblois, the young woman from Boston who had so flatly rejected him as a suitor, was very much on his mind. He wrote her again, imploring her to change her decision. But when she replied, it was to tell him she wanted none of his attentions.

Arnold went on to New Haven, where he was given a tremendous ovation by his old command, the Guards, whom he had led to Cambridge after Lexington and Concord. An eighteen-gun salute was fired in his honor. And his sister, Hannah, and his boys were overjoyed to see him again.

After a short stay in New Haven, Arnold was at Valley Forge on May 21, reporting for duty to General Washington. He was rid of his crutch, but his wound was still giving him much trouble. The commander in chief's esteem for him knew no bounds. Washington saw that it would be a long time, if ever, before Arnold could return to action in the field, but somehow he must be suitably rewarded. He felt he could bestow no higher honor on the hero of Saratoga than the command of Philadelphia.

The opportunity to give him this post was a result of the British army's recent evacuation of the city in mid-June 1778. The British had captured Philadelphia on September 26, 1777, following Howe's victory over Washington at the battle of Brandywine. After forcing the Continental Congress to flee the city, the British had set up headquarters there, with Howe in command.

Howe and his junior officers thoroughly enjoyed their tour of duty in Philadelphia. Scores of wealthy Tories who had fled the city while it was in American hands returned from their country estates to their abandoned fine town houses. The winter of 1777–78 was one long round of balls, dinners, theatrical performances and other social events.

Howe was an aristocrat, an able officer when he used his

military talents, popular with his men and one who loved social activity. He gave many parties at his headquarters in the splendid Richard Penn mansion and in turn was feted by the Tory elite. Howe's aide, Major John André, was a handsome, gallant young officer with a genius for organizing all sorts of social affairs. He arranged popular theatrical productions, designing scenery and costumes, writing some of the plays and acting in some. When Howe left Philadelphia, André staged a farewell party known as the *Mischianza*, the most gorgeous pageant, dinner and entertainment the city had ever seen.

André was irresistible to the young ladies of Philadelphia, especially to the three charming and beautiful daughters of Judge Edward Shippen, a prominent and wealthy moderate Loyalist. They and the other belles of the city sorely missed John André when the British left under orders from London to evacuate. Possession of the American capital was then of doubtful desirability to the British. The French alliance with America had been achieved, and French naval power might bottle up Howe by sea in Philadelphia, with the Americans blockading him by land. Sir Henry Clinton, now supreme commander of the British armies in America, decided Howe's army should leave before that could happen and that the British would do better to concentrate their efforts upon campaigns farther north.

Benedict Arnold did his best to replace both Howe and André. Before he left Washington's camp, he took the oath of allegiance to the new United States of America, required of all officers of the Continental Army. He was to make a mockery of it, yet his arrival in Philadelphia was an occasion for great rejoicing by its patriot residents. He rode into the city on June 19 in a splendid coach through streets jammed with cheering people. Bells pealed, drums thundered and a thirteen-gun salute was fired to the new military commander. The Tories who had been strongly loyal to Howe fled once more, but a good many residents who had accepted and even supported the British occupation remained and were tolerated, including the Shippen family. Patriots who had left the city returned.

Arnold's popularity with the patriots was short-lived. The day after his arrival he established martial law in the city. For a week many shops were closed so that whatever British imports, Loyalist property and other matériel needed by the army could be taken from these establishments. The closings were perfectly normal procedure, but Arnold's action caused a storm of protest among Philadelphians.

As time went on, the people's dislike of Arnold increased. They resented his moving into Howe's magnificent headquarters in the Richard Penn house, his arrogance and his way of life, since he immediately began to live beyond his means. Nor did it please the patriots that socially prominent people with Loyalist leanings who had associated with Howe were now accepted at Arnold's social affairs and in turn entertained him.

Arnold got himself deeper into the bad graces of the patriots when in order to obtain money for his high living he took part in some rather suspicious commercial enterprises. One involved the purchase, using government funds, of goods not needed by the army and their sale. Nothing was definitely proved against Arnold, but it was believed that some of the profits went into his pocket. His part in some private shipping ventures prompted his enemies' efforts to find a way to charge him with serious violations of his office. However, in at least one of these deals Arnold lost heavily.

He then got into trouble with staunch Philadelphia patriots in an entirely different way. Margaret Shippen, better known as Peggy, was the youngest, fairest and most charming of Edward Shippen's daughters. Major André had shown her a great deal of attention, and she deeply regretted his absence. Now Arnold attempted to take André's place in her affections.

He met Peggy Shippen during the summer of 1778, and in September he wrote her a letter so much like the second one he had sent to Betsy Deblois that it was practically a copy. Even though she was only eighteen and Arnold thirty-seven, Peggy was intrigued; he was the most prominent man in Philadelphia. She made no quick decision, and the courtship went on for several months. Peggy's father did not favor the match, even after Arnold wrote him asking for Peggy's hand, but the general was not to be denied. In time Judge Shippen gave his consent.

Arnold acquired Mount Pleasant, an imposing estate on six acres of land, for his bride-to-be. Peggy Shippen and Benedict Arnold were married on April 8, 1779, in the Shippen mansion. She was the second Peggy to become Arnold's wife.

Arnold's troubles piled up soon after his marriage. Although he was the supreme military commander in Philadelphia, the government of the United States and that of the commonwealth of Pennsylvania were located there. He had enemies among both. One was Joseph Reed, president of the Pennsylvania Council.

In February 1779 Reed brought before Congress several charges of misconduct against Arnold. Four of them concerned his money-making activities; the others, including a

charge of favoritism toward Loyalists, were of little importance. Angrily Arnold demanded an immediate investigation.
In March a congressional committee recommended that he
be cleared of all the charges, but Reed persisted, and in April
Congress ordered Arnold's court-martial on the four more
serious counts.

Some of Arnold's commercial activities were probably dis-
honest, but his accusers had little evidence to prove it. However, the court-martial sentenced him to be reprimanded on
two of the charges. It was a distasteful duty for Washington
and his reprimand was gentle, but Arnold was outraged
nonetheless.

Arnold was sick of his troubles with his enemies, and because his wounded leg still troubled him, he had no chance
of returning to action in the field. In Philadelphia he was little
more than a civilian, although a powerful one. In spite of his
vivacious and lovely new wife, whom he adored, the luxury
of their life and the social whirl of which they were the
center, he was bored.

Money was his chief worry in the spring of 1779. The
Arnolds were still living in the Richard Penn house. For the
time being, at least, he decided to rent out Mount Pleasant,
since it cost a great deal to keep up. And there were the
additional expenses of the many parties the Arnolds gave, fine
clothes and the fees to keep one of Arnold's sons at a private
school.

Money was the god Arnold had always worshiped, and he
felt that with more of it he could solve all his difficulties. His
trading deals had brought him some profit but not enough,
and with his enemies watching every move he made, it was
next to impossible to do more trading, shady or honest. There

was one way left to get a lot of money. Arnold knew the British would pay handsomely for helpful military information. It was then that Arnold decided on his treason.

The first thing he needed was a secret contact with General Clinton in New York City. He found it in Joseph Stansbury, who ran a glass and china shop in Philadelphia. He was a Loyalist who did not openly proclaim it. He had remained in the city during Howe's occupation, living quietly and becoming acquainted with the British general, who liked and trusted him. When the Americans took over the city, Stansbury had taken the oath of allegiance but remained a staunch ally of the British cause. He was tolerated by the Americans as harmless.

Arnold learned of Stansbury's true allegiance and sought his acquaintance. He moved with extreme caution. He had to be absolutely sure that Stansbury was trustworthy before exposing his plans. In time he was convinced that the shopkeeper was indeed fully reliable. One story has it that Peggy Arnold had learned through Major André that Stansbury could be depended upon.

How much did Peggy Shippen Arnold know of her husband's treason? It has been proved that she did know and assisted him in it, but there is no proof that she influenced him to turn traitor. She certainly had a part in the early phases of the treason.

Once Arnold had told Stansbury, under a strict oath of secrecy, what he intended to do, the shopkeeper went to New York. He brought Clinton an offer from Arnold either to join the British army or to cooperate in some way of advantage to Clinton.

In New York Stansbury conferred with André, now aide-de-camp to Clinton. André talked with the general and told Stansbury that Arnold's assistance would be welcome. If the traitor could manage to turn over a good-sized number of American troops to the British, he would be handsomely rewarded.

For communication a secret code was set up. André was to begin a correspondence with one of his many friends among the belles of Philadelphia, Peggy Chew. The Chews were outright Loyalists who had a fine mansion in Germantown on the fringe of Philadelphia. Peggy Chew and Peggy Shippen Arnold had been close friends since girlhood.

The letters would be innocent enough, simply reminiscences of the good times André and Peggy Chew had enjoyed during the British occupation. However, between the lines of the communications would be messages written in invisible ink that could be revealed by treating the paper with acid or exposing it to heat. Peggy Chew was to turn the letters over to Peggy Arnold.

Risky as it was, the plan worked. Arnold forwarded bits of information he could obtain about Washington's army. It was not enough, however. Arnold was prepared to give greater assistance if he could. Meanwhile he tried to pin Clinton down about how much he would receive if he delivered a body of American troops to the British.

Clinton evaded a definite offer. Finally Arnold received a suggestion that he resume active service, obtain a command, allow himself to be surprised, cut off by the British and surrender five or six thousand American troops. For this he would be richly rewarded, although Clinton did not say by just how much.

Arnold was annoyed by Clinton's vagueness. Then André

wrote suggesting that he obtain an accurate plan of the fort at West Point. The fort was a strong key to control of the Hudson Valley and the British wanted it. Arnold, without a specific offer of how much the British would pay, made no reply, and for some time there were no more negotiations.

He had more troubles in Philadelphia. Merchants, financiers and other war profiteers were becoming rich, but the value of American paper money was declining rapidly. Prices rose and the people of the city were the victims of inflation. A mob of workmen, riffraff from the waterfront and some discontented militia rioted against the profiteers. Arnold himself went to the scene, drew two pistols and threatened to fire on the mob, which then dispersed.

There was one pleasant event during these trying days. On March 19, 1780, Arnold's fourth son, Edward, was born. General and Mrs. Washington sent personal congratulations to the Arnolds. At the same time, however, affairs in the household were not going smoothly. Hannah Arnold had come to take care of the new baby, and Peggy Arnold did not get along well with her husband's sometimes domineering and sharp-tongued sister.

Money was still Arnold's chief difficulty. The Board of Treasury reported that he owed the government $70,000 in connection with expenditures made during the Canadian campaign. Arnold fought the demand so fiercely that the alleged debt was reduced to $2,328 in hard money. Arnold could not raise even this amount, and the debt was not paid until after his treason, when all his property was seized.

Arnold decided to resume negotiations with the British on West Point. Apparently he conferred with General Schuyler, then a delegate to the Continental Congress, and suggested himself for the West Point command. Schuyler, who thought highly of Arnold, had a talk with Washington about it.

Arnold was convinced that the commander in chief would give him the post. He reopened his correspondence with Clinton, saying that he must have £10,000 to compensate him if the American government seized his property once his treason was known, and £100 a year to make up for the pay he would lose as an American general. As for West Point, he said that if he could turn it over to the British, £20,000 would be a cheap price for it.

Washington wanted to reward Arnold with a better post than West Point, however. The commander in chief felt that Arnold was now in shape to take the field. On August 1 he named him to command the Continental Army's left wing, as high an honor as he could bestow. By that time Arnold was too deeply enmeshed in the plot to accept the offer. He went to headquarters and protested that the condition of his leg would not permit active service. Washington then gave him the West Point command.

By August 5, 1780, Arnold had been relieved of the Philadelphia command and had set up headquarters at the house of Colonel Beverley Robinson, across the Hudson and about two miles downriver from West Point. Soon afterward Peggy joined him with baby Edward.

On August 24 a letter from André contained an offer of £20,000 to surrender West Point with all its artillery and stores and 3,000 men. Arnold wrote back accepting it.

He then sought a trustworthy agent by whom he could exchange messages with British headquarters. The man he found, Joshua Hett Smith, lived down the river near King's Ferry. While Howe was in command in New York City,

Smith had sent him reports from Hudson Valley spies and had proved reliable and useful to the British general.

Arnold felt he must have a meeting with André, Clinton's representative, in carrying out the plot. As a result the British sloop-of-war *Vulture*, stationed at Spuyten Duyvil, off the northern end of Manhattan Island, sailed up to King's Ferry with André aboard. Joshua Hett Smith was rowed out to the British man-of-war. He carried a document signed by Arnold authorizing him and a Mr. John Anderson (actually André) to "pass and repass the guards near King's Ferry at all times."

André came ashore with Smith and met Arnold alone in the woods. The conference lasted until about four in the morning. Exactly what the two discussed is not known, but it concerned details of the West Point fort's surrender. Arnold dared not risk sending André back to the *Vulture* by daylight, since he would be carrying incriminating documents, including a detailed plan of the West Point defenses. The two went to Smith's house, where André was to wait until the following night before returning to the British warship.

Fate had other plans in store for André. Colonel James Livingston, in command of the American forces in the vicinity, saw the *Vulture* in the river. He had two cannon mounted within range of her on the east bank of the river and opened fire on the warship. Before the *Vulture* could unlimber her guns, she was hit several times and forced to turn tail and head down the Hudson.

Arnold, watching from a window of Smith's house, was appalled. André was in deep trouble. Clinton had ordered him not to go in disguise, not to pass the American lines and to carry no papers. He was inside the lines now and his British uniform would certainly make his capture certain if he encountered American troops on his way back by land. Yet by land he must go, carrying the documents that could reveal the plot, all in Arnold's handwriting.

Smith gave the British major a beaver hat and one of his own coats to wear over his uniform. Arnold wrote a pass for him under the name of John Anderson and told him to destroy the documents and plan of West Point if he was intercepted.

At sunset André, accompanied by Smith and a black servant, rode off. At King's Ferry they crossed to the east bank of the river. Between eight and nine o'clock they were challenged by an American military patrol under Captain Ebenezer Boyd. Smith told him they were going to White Plains to get intelligence for Arnold. Boyd inspected their credentials and told them to take a roundabout route since the main road to Tarrytown was infested with Tory guerrillas. He also insisted they spend the night at a neighboring house.

The three rode on the next morning, stopping for breakfast at Pine's Bridge over the Croton River. Here Smith's courage deserted him. He told André he would have to go on from there alone.

On a little bridge over a brook André encountered three American militiamen lying in wait at the far end of the bridge. They were rascals, out to rob anyone they met, friend or foe. One of them, John Paulding, was wearing a British army coat. André thought he was among friends and told Paulding he was a British officer. Paulding then said he and his companions were Americans. André produced Arnold's pass but Paulding did not bother to look at it. If he had, he said afterward, he would have allowed André to go.

Instead, the three men took his watch and the small amount

of money he had with him and then decided he must have
some concealed valuables. They ordered André to strip. The
major first told the men they would find themselves in trouble
with Arnold if they did not let him go. When this failed,
he offered them a bribe. They might have accepted if they
had not found the concealed papers in André's boots. Paulding then decided the prisoner should be turned over to Lieutenant Colonel John Jameson at North Castle.

There André came very close to escaping. Jameson was
neither an intelligent man nor a capable officer. He knew
Arnold was expecting a John Anderson of New York, so he
was about to let him proceed. He gave "Anderson" a letter
to Arnold telling about the papers the major had been carrying. André, of course, would simply have gone on to safety
inside the nearby British lines, and Arnold's treason would not
have been discovered in time.

Luckily, Jameson's superior, Colonel Benjamin Tallmadge,
returned just then from patrol. He took a different view of
what had happened. He ordered that André be held. Jameson
argued that "Mr. Anderson" was doubtless going to give
Arnold valuable intelligence about the British. Tallmadge allowed the letter to be sent on to Arnold at West Point, but
he dispatched the documents to General Washington. The
commander in chief was then on his way back from Hartford,
Connecticut, after an important conference with two high-
ranking French officers, Lieutenant General de Rochambeau
and Admiral de Ternay. They had discussed an attack on the
British in New York City.

Meanwhile Joshua Hett Smith had gone to Arnold's headquarters and told him André had passed through the American
lines. That was Saturday, September 23. Arnold waited anx-

iously over the weekend, expecting word from Clinton by Monday.

Washington had not received the documents found on André when he spent Sunday night at Fishkill. He planned to visit West Point the next day. On Monday morning he sent two aides ahead to tell the Arnolds he would be there for breakfast.

But for a delay when Washington turned off the main road to inspect two redoubts on the river bank, Benedict Arnold would almost certainly have been caught and hanged. Washington sent two young officers ahead to tell Peggy not to wait breakfast.

When the officers arrived at Arnold's headquarters, he courteously asked them to breakfast. Just then a messenger arrived with the letter from Jameson telling of André's capture and the papers discovered on him. Arnold was staggered but he quickly recovered his composure.

Peggy Arnold was upstairs at the time. Arnold excused himself and went up to tell her the worst had happened and that he must get away at once. He then went downstairs, summoned Major Daniel Franks, one of his aides, and told him to say to Washington when he arrived that he had gone to West Point and would return in about an hour. Then his horse was quickly saddled and Arnold galloped madly over a short cut to the landing, where a boat was always ready for his use. He told the oarsmen to row with all speed for the *Vulture*, which had come back upriver, adding that he must get back as soon as possible to meet General Washington.

The commander in chief arrived half an hour later. Peggy Arnold sent word downstairs that she was ill. When Washington heard the message from Arnold, so great was his trust in the traitor that he suspected nothing and sat down to breakfast. Afterward he went over to West Point.

He was shocked to find the defenses in a very neglected state. He asked for Arnold and was told the fort's commander had not been there. Washington sensed that something was wrong, but he still could not believe Arnold was responsible for it. He went back to Robinson House across the river.

Then Colonel Alexander Hamilton arrived with the papers captured on André. One glance at them revealed Arnold's treason. Washington ordered Hamilton and another officer to try to catch Arnold. They were too late.

The deed was done, although West Point was saved. Perhaps the best summing-up of the impact it would have on the army and all of America is what Washington said to the Marquis de Lafayette, who was with his party: "Whom can we trust now?"

ELEVEN

The Last Years

They hanged John André. A board of inquiry headed by General Greene questioned the British major in Tappan, where he was imprisoned. He gave detailed and honest answers. Since his uniform had been concealed under the coat Smith had given him, the board had no choice but to have him executed as a spy. Greene wept when he pronounced the sentence. André asked to be shot as a soldier, but Washington was compelled by military custom to send a spy to the gallows.

The hanging, set for October 1, was delayed a day at Clinton's request. Apparently the general did make some effort to save the man he had sent to his death. There is a story, not proved, that Clinton rejected an American offer to exchange André for Arnold. André went courageously to his death on October 2, 1780. Not only the British but all America mourned him as a brave young officer who had been merely Clinton's cat's-paw in the negotiations and had been caught while the American traitor escaped.

As for Arnold, once he was safe aboard the *Vulture*, he wrote an impassioned letter to Washington asking that Peggy be spared any insult or injury and that she either be allowed to go to Philadelphia or come to him. She was, he untruthfully declared, "as good and innocent as an angel and is incapable of doing wrong."

When she was taken into custody at the Robinson house, she was hysterical, raving and weeping uncontrollably. Washington and his officers were at that time convinced she was innocent. The commander in chief respected Arnold's request, and she was treated with every kindness. On September 27 Major Franks was sent to escort her to Philadelphia.

Meanwhile the *Vulture* bore Arnold to New York City. For the most part his welcome by the British was cool. Many of the younger officers who had been André's friends would have nothing to do with the traitor. New York Loyalists treated him politely but guardedly; the treason had been so cold-blooded that even they would not fully accept it. Only Clinton and royal Chief Justice William Smith, Joshua Hett Smith's brother, were genuinely friendly. Clinton's kind treatment seems odd, considering that Arnold had failed to turn West Point over to the British and André had been executed.

Among American patriots feeling ran high against the traitor. He was hanged or burned in effigy in Boston, Philadelphia, Providence and other places. In his native Connecticut rage against him was even greater. An image of him was dragged through the streets of New Haven. The dummy was seated in a chair and had two faces to symbolize double-dealing. In its hand was a letter, supposedly from Satan, saying he could never do a more evil thing and must hang himself. Behind the chair was the devil, all in black, shaking a purse in his left hand while the other held a pitchfork, poised to send Arnold into hell.

No records indicate what Hannah thought of her brother's treason, but when he needed help later on, she stood by him.

As for Arnold's sons by both marriages, all were too young to have a clear understanding of what had happened, the oldest being only about eleven at the time of the treason.

In New York Arnold took a house near Clinton's headquarters. He lost no time in claiming the reward he felt was due him. Soon after his arrival he told Clinton that £10,000 was not too much to compensate him for all he had been through.

Clinton did reward Arnold promptly. Less than two weeks later the traitor was paid £6,000 along with £350 of expense money. Today that amount would be worth close to $100,000. Arnold was also given a colonel's commission in the regular British army at £450 a year, to continue at half pay after retirement as long as he lived. While serving in America as a provincial brigadier general, he would get an additional £200 a year until peace was concluded.

Nor were these sums his only reward. George III issued a warrant for an annual pension to Peggy Arnold of £500. Obviously the king appreciated her part in the betrayal. In fact, Clinton said that she had performed services that were "very meritorious."

There was more. Any of Arnold's sons who survived him received a pension that would bring them £80 a year. Arnold's three sons by his first wife were given commissions (salaried but honorary until they were old enough to serve) in the British army, to receive half pay after the war. Altogether, treason did pay in Arnold's case.

He tried to justify what he had done. He issued two proclamations, one "To the Inhabitants of America" and the other "A Proclamation to the Officers and Soldiers of the Continental Army." In the first Arnold claimed that the American patriots had been misled into rebellion and that the inhabitants of their allied country, France, were not free themselves. The latter charge was true enough, but it did not change the Americans' views. The address to the army was in much the same vein.

Arnold even tried to convince Lord Germain that the Continental Army soldiers could be bribed to give up by offering them half pay for seven and a half years after the war and generous amounts of land if they would come over to the British. Washington himself, said Arnold, could be induced to join his enemy in return for a British title. This scheme was tried but brought only a handful of Americans to the British. And Washington's greatest desire was to catch Arnold and hang him.

During this time Peggy Arnold and little Edward were in Philadelphia. She found the city hostile. The newspapers printed items based on Arnold's seized papers that threw suspicion on her as her husband's accomplice in the treason. Friends of the old days in Philadelphia ignored her, and there was public demand for her banishment. On October 27, 1781, the Pennsylvania Council ordered her to leave the city within two weeks because her presence there was dangerous to the public safety.

The Shippen family fought the order vigorously. Judge Shippen wanted Peggy never to rejoin her husband. The efforts were of no avail, however, and Peggy and her little son reached New York on November 14. She can be blamed for her part in the treason, but her loyalty to Arnold can never be questioned.

Arnold hoped to get into action with the British. His chance came in 1781, when General Cornwallis was trying to subdue

South and North Carolina and then advance into Virginia to meet Washington and destroy the American army. To aid Cornwallis, Clinton sent Arnold on a raiding expedition to Virginia.

For all his friendliness, Clinton does not seem to have trusted Arnold fully. The general ordered him to consult with two subordinate lieutenant colonels attached to the force before attempting an important move. Arnold, determined to show Clinton he could accomplish a relatively small mission and win command of a bigger one, accepted the humiliation.

Before he sailed for Virginia, Arnold barely escaped capture by the Americans. He had been trying to organize a corps of American deserters. Major "Light Horse Harry" Lee sent Sergeant John Champe and another enlisted man over to the British, where they were accepted into Arnold's group. Champe and his accomplice were to sneak into Arnold's quarters at night, seize him and take him by boat to Hoboken, New Jersey, where Lee would be waiting. The daring plan might have succeeded if Champe's unit had not been ordered to sail south on the very night the kidnaping was to take place.

Arnold sailed from New York on December 21, 1780, with 1,600 British regulars, Hessians and Tory volunteers. Landing at Hampton Roads, he marched to Richmond, where he burned and plundered many warehouses filled with valuable tobacco, as well as public and private property. Other towns were also devastated before Arnold, following orders, seized and fortified Portsmouth. Washington tried hard but in vain to catch and hang the traitor.

Although Arnold had done well on this mission, it did not improve his military ambitions. He did share in the loot that was taken, however. Just how much he got is not definitely known, but one figure sets his profit at £2,068. In the spring he was recalled to New York. The summer of 1781 passed with no new assignment, and the most pleasurable event was the birth of another son, James.

Arnold then devised a plan for an expedition against New London, Connecticut, to divert American forces in that direction and help Cornwallis. With Arnold in command, the expedition sailed from New York on November 4 with about 1,700 troops.

In his assault on New London he was the old Arnold in action, letting nothing stand in the way of complete victory. Two forts, Trumbull and Griswold, guarded the town. Fort Trumbull surrendered, but Griswold resisted. Arnold sent a division against it. Although the Connecticut defenders fought fiercely, they had to surrender. The fort's commander handed his sword to the leader of the British division, who instantly drove it through the American officer's body, killing him. The British regulars, Hessians and Tories then began a massacre of the fort's garrison. They killed 85 men, wounded 60 and captured the few that remained. Arnold and the rest of his troops had gone on into New London, so this shocking violation of the rules of war was not his doing, but the responsibility for it was his.

In New London his troops began a wanton destruction of the town, burning warehouses, shipyards, wharves, public buildings and inhabitants' houses. Then they crossed the Thames River and did the same to the little town of Groton.

This expedition was Arnold's farewell to active military service. It did not succeed in drawing American troops to the area but only increased American hatred of him. Cornwallis's surrender at Yorktown followed on October 19. Arnold, back in New York, favored continuing the struggle. He obtained permission to go to England and present his ideas on how victory might yet be won.

Arnold sailed for England in a warship on December 15, 1781. Peggy followed in a regular packet ship with her two young sons and her maids. Hannah stayed in New Haven with Arnold's three oldest boys, now finished with school.

Arnold received better treatment in London than in New York. British Whig newspapers and members of that political party, which was opposed to British efforts to subdue the American colonies, criticized the traitor, but Lord George Germain's attitude was respectful, and Sir Guy Carleton, then in London, and Sir Walter Stirling were friendly and presented him to King George III. The king, who refused to give up hope of winning the war, liked Arnold and asked for his ideas on continuing the struggle. Peggy was presented to Queen Charlotte, who liked her so much that she asked her ladies of the court to pay special attention to Arnold's wife.

The traitor then wrote "Thoughts on the American War." He said that most Americans were saddled with backbreaking taxation and favored reunion with Britain, that mutiny and desertion had spread all through the Continental Army and other outrageously false statements. Since the French had left after Yorktown, said Arnold, now was the time to strike before they could come back. All this the king swallowed as truth. Nevertheless, the Revolution ended with the signing of the Treaty of Paris on September 3, 1783, and the United States was forever free of British control.

Arnold's thoughts then turned to making money. He decided the American continent offered the best opportunity.

In Canada, at St. John, New Brunswick, the British government had established a settlement for Loyalists who had fled the United States. Arnold bought and fitted out a brig, the *Lord Middleton*, and in October 1785 sailed for St. John, leaving Peggy and the rest of their family in London. Two children, a girl born in 1783 and a boy in 1784, had died, but another daughter, born in 1785, had survived, so there were now two boys and a girl with Peggy.

Arnold was much encouraged when he reached St. John. The settlement there had been chartered only six months earlier. Its chief industries were lumbering and fishing, and it seemed ripe for development. Arnold bought a store, took a Loyalist partner, Munson Hoyt, and resumed his old business as a merchant–shipowner.

Although he put all his energies into the business, Arnold's hopes of becoming rich did not materialize. The brig foundered in a storm, and he bought another, a new one named *Lord Sheffield*. Then, leaving his partner in charge of the store, he made a trading voyage to the West Indies. From there he sailed to England and brought Peggy and the children to St. John, where he bought a house. Hannah and his two older sons came there from New Haven.

Hoping to make more money, Arnold established trading posts, where he dealt in lumber and provisions, at St. John, Campobello Island and the capital of the province, Fredericton. He especially liked Fredericton and purchased a house in which he stayed whenever he was there.

Business did not improve for Arnold. He lent money to several men with whom he had dealings, and they had trouble repaying the debts. He put another vessel, the *George*, into service, but strong competition and high insurance rates reduced his profits. Also the infamy of his treason followed him to St. John. Even the Loyalists distrusted him and disliked him for his arrogance.

His bad luck continued. In 1788 he made a trading voyage to London. There he insured his warehouse, its contents and the stock of the St. John store for a total of £6,000. On America's Independence Day, July 4, 1788, the warehouse and the goods in it were destroyed by fire. Although Arnold was in England then, a rumor sprang up that he had had the fire set, and the insurance company refused to pay. In time he got the money, but the rumor that he had had a hand in the fire persisted and his unpopularity increased in St. John. In 1789 he rented his house there and moved to Fredericton.

Arnold's troubles mounted. In 1790 his partner, Hoyt, charged that the Arnolds had robbed him of £700. Arnold brought suit against Hoyt, seeking £5,000 in damages for slander. During the trial he produced promissory notes proving that Hoyt owed him nearly £2,000. Arnold won the suit, but the judge seems to have been no friend of his. The traitor was awarded the absurd sum of two shillings and sixpence.

During this time Peggy Arnold went back to Philadelphia to visit the Shippen family. She arrived in the fall of 1789 but was so coldly treated and neglected by her old friends that she left for the last time in April 1790.

Dislike of Arnold increased in St. John, to which he had returned. People still believed Hoyt's claim that Arnold had robbed him. Incredible as it seems, a mob of Loyalists gathered in front of Arnold's house and burned an effigy of him labeled "Traitor!"

That was the beginning of the end for the Arnolds in New Brunswick. It was not until 1792, however, that Arnold was able to sell his property there, auction off his household goods and sail for England with Peggy and their children, including a new son, George, who had been born in 1787. Hannah returned to New Haven but eventually went to live in Canada with two of Arnold's sons by his first marriage.

In London Arnold sought another appointment in the British army but to no avail. He then went back to trading and privateering in the West Indies. During this period he fought a duel with the Earl of Lansdale, who had made slurring remarks on Arnold's character in the House of Lords. The duel took place on July 1, 1792. Pistols were the weapons, and it was agreed that both men should fire at a signal from Lansdale's second. Arnold did so and missed, but his opponent refused to fire. Arnold and his second demanded that Lansdale fire or take back his insulting words. The earl finally apologized and Arnold, his honor vindicated, went back to Peggy, who had been beside herself with worry.

Arnold's conduct in the duel brought him so much praise that he tried for a government appointment. Clinton recommended him for such a post, but the prime minister did nothing about it.

Arnold then bought another ship to resume his trading, but she was captured by a French privateer. He then sailed in another vessel to the West Indies to buy sugar. Britain and France were at war again, and when Arnold went to Guadeloupe, which had been under British control, he found that the French had taken it. Although he landed, claiming to be an American, the French put him aboard a prison ship. He had managed to conceal his money and bribed guards to let him escape to a British warship.

When Arnold returned to England in the summer of 1795, he found Peggy ill of a nervous disorder. He was saddened again when his oldest son, Benedict, a British army officer, was wounded in action in the West Indies and died.

Three times Arnold tried unsuccessfully for another military appointment. However, he did make a claim as a former Loyalist officer for a land grant in Upper Canada. He, Peggy and their sons were given 13,400 acres and were exempted from the usual requirement that the owners settle on the land.

Arnold was ill now and he sensed that he did not have long to live. Thinking of his family's welfare, he plunged into privateering in a desperate effort to make a large sum of money. Privateers were privately owned ships commissioned in wartime to prey upon enemy shipping or vessels trading with the enemy. Actually it was little less than government-approved piracy, with profits from the loot divided proportionally among the ship's company and the owners. Again Arnold was unlucky. Unscrupulous captains of his ships are believed to have cheated him of as much as £50,000. When he did get his share of the £20,000 profit from a Spanish prize, his many creditors immediately claimed it, for as usual he was deep in debt.

These last years were the most unhappy ones of Arnold's life. Nothing had gone well for him financially, and Peggy, to whom he remained deeply devoted, was almost an invalid. Arnold often had to take her out of London for country air or the healing waters of medicinal springs.

Arnold himself had developed an asthmatic cough. It grew

steadily worse until, by early 1801, he seldom got more than two hours' sleep a night. His good leg was swollen from dropsy; the one wounded at Quebec and Saratoga throbbed constantly, and he had to use a cane. His trim military bearing was gone; his shoulders were bony and stooped, his complexion sallow and his flesh flabby.

As the end of Arnold's days approached, he was a financially ruined man, with creditors constantly hounding him. Peggy managed to pay off his debts, but there was little left except for Arnold's pension and her own.

By June 8, 1801, Arnold was critically ill. The asthma was choking him and his throat was so inflamed that he could not swallow. On June 10 he became delirious. Now and then he recovered his senses enough to ask blessings on Peggy and his children. At about 6:30 A.M. on June 12, Benedict Arnold died quietly.

They buried him in the crypt of St. Mary's Church in Battersea, a borough of London. Only the briefest of items in the newspapers told of his death. His loving wife survived him by only about two years.

Here was a man who, after the battle of Saratoga, had had everything to live for. He was then a national hero. Great Revolutionary generals thought highly of him—the commander in chief, Greene, Lafayette and others. Even after the unfortunate experience in Philadelphia he could have gone on to new glory in the highest command Washington could give him. Once the Revolution was over, Arnold could have retired to New Haven. With his business ability he might have gained the fortune he craved so intensely and have lived out his life in prosperity with Peggy.

Arnold's greed for money was the chief trait in his character that drove him to treason, rather than his grievances against his enemies in the Continental Congress and the army. He threw away his future for gold that turned to lead in his hands and made his name an everlasting symbol for treachery.

Truly, Natanis's supposed predictions were realized in every respect. When Benedict Arnold soared highest and his wings brushed the sky, the arrow that pierced his heart was released.

Bibliography

Allen, Ethan. *A Narrative of Colonel Ethan Allen's Captivity.* Burlington, Vt.: Chauncey Goodrich, 1846.

Arnold, Isaac N. *The Life of Benedict Arnold.* Chicago: Jansen McClurg, 1880.

Boatner, Mark M., III. *Encyclopedia of the American Revolution.* New York: McKay, 1966.

Boylan, Bryan Richard. *Benedict Arnold, the Dark Eagle.* New York: Norton, 1973.

Bradley, A. C. *Lord Dorchester.* Toronto: Morang & Co., 1907.

Caulkins, Francis Mainwaring. *History of Norwich, Connecticut.* Norwich: Published by the author, 1866.

Davies, Bladwen. *The Storied Streets of Quebec.* Montreal: Louis Carrier & Co., 1929.

Decker, Malcolm. *Benedict Arnold, Son of the Havens.* Tarrytown, N.Y.: William Abbate, 1932.

Dupuy, R. Ernest and Dupuy, Trevor N. *The Compact History of the Revolution.* New York: Hawthorn, 1963.

Fiske, John. *The American Revolution.* Boston: Houghton Mifflin, 1891.

Fitzgerald, John C., ed. *The Writings of George Washington from the Original Manuscript Sources.* Washington: Government Printing Office, 1937.

Forbes, Esther. *Paul Revere and the World He Lived In.* Boston: Houghton Mifflin, 1942.

Force, Peter. *American Archives.* Washington: M. St. Clair and Peter Force, 1833.

Gale, George. *Historic Tales of Old Quebec.* Quebec: Telegraph Printing Co., 1932.

Gottschalk, Louis. *Lafayette and the Close of the American Revolution.* Chicago: University of Chicago Press, 1942.

Higginbotham, Don. *The War of American Independence.* New York: Macmillan, 1971.

Hill, George Canning. *Benedict Arnold.* New York: 1884.

Hudleston, F. J. *Gentleman Johnny Burgoyne.* Garden City, N.Y.: Garden City Publishing Co., 1927.

Lefferts, Charles M. *Uniforms of the American, Canadian, British, French and German Armies in the War of the American Revolution.* New York: New York Historical Society, 1926.

Lemoine, J. M. *Quebec, Past and Present.* Quebec: Augustin Coté et Cie., 1876.

Lengyel, Cornel. *I, Benedict Arnold.* Garden City: Doubleday, 1960.

Lodge, Henry Cabot, ed. *The Works of Alexander Hamilton.* New York: Putnam, 1886.

Lossing, Benson J. *The American Revolution and the War of 1812.* New York: New York Book Concern, 1875.

Miller, John C. *Origins of the American Revolution.* Boston: Little, Brown, 1943.

Moore, Frank. *Diary of the American Revolution.* New York: Scribner, 1865.

Newton, Charles Bertram, and Treat, Edwin Bryant. *Outline for Review, American History.* New York: American Book Co., 1921.

Newton, Earle. *The Vermont Story.* Montpelier: Vermont Historical Society, 1949.

Paine, Lauren. *Benedict Arnold, Hero and Traitor.* London: Robert Hale, 1965.

Parker, Gilbert, and Bryan, Claude G. *Old Quebec.* New York: Macmillan, 1904.

Parkman, Francis. *Montcalm and Wolfe.* Boston: Little, Brown, 1910.

Roberts, Kenneth, ed. *March to Quebec.* New York: Doubleday, Doran, 1938.

Sargent, Winthrop. *The Life of Major John André.* New York: D. Appleton, 1871.

Sellers, Charles Coleman. *Benedict Arnold, the Proud Warrior.* New York: Minton, Balch, 1930.

Sherwin, Oscar. *Benedict Arnold, Patriot and Traitor.* New York: The Century Company, 1931.

Smith, Justin H. *Our Struggle for the Fourteenth Colony— Canada and the American Revolution.* New York: Putnam, 1907.

Sullivan, Edward Dean. *Benedict Arnold, Military Racketeer.* New York: Vanguard Press, 1932.

Taylor, John George. *Some New Light on the Later Life and Last Resting Place of Benedict Arnold.* London: G. White, 1931.

Thayer, Theodore. *Nathanael Greene.* New York: Twayne, 1960.

Tillotson, Harry Stanton. The *Exquisite Exile, the Life and Fortunes of Mrs. Benedict Arnold.* Boston: Lothrop, Lee & Shepard, 1932.

Van de Water, Frederic F. *Reluctant Republic.* New York: John Day, 1941.

Van Doren, Carl. *Secret History of the American Revolution.* New York: Viking, 1941.

Van Schaak, Henry Cruger. *Memoirs of the Life of Henry Van Schaak.* Chicago, A. C. McClurg & Co., 1892.

Wade, Herbert Treadwell. *A Brief History of the Colonial Wars in America.* New York: Society of Colonial Wars in the State of New York, 1948.

Wallace, Willard M. *Traitorous Hero.* New York: Harper & Row, 1970.

Ward, Christopher. *The War of the Revolution.* New York: Macmillan, 1952.

Winsor, Justin, ed. *The Memorial History of Boston.* Boston: James R. Osgood & Co., 1881.

Wood, William. "The Father of British Canada." *Chronicles of Canada,* Vol. 12. Toronto: Glasgow, Brook & Co., 1916.

Index